Numerical Questions
for
Standard Grade
Physics

Lyn Robinson

Principal Teacher of Physics

Williamwood High School, Clarkston

Published by
Chemcord
16 Inch Keith
East Kilbride
Glasgow

ISBN 1 870570 63 4

© **Robinson , 1997**
First reprint 2002

All rights reserved. No part of this publication may be reproduced or transmitted in any form or by any means, electronic or mechanical, including photocopy, recording, or any information storage and retrieval system, without permission in writing from the publisher or under licence from the Copyright Licensing Agency.

Printed by Bell and Bain Ltd, Glasgow

CONTENTS

BASIC MATHEMATICS — 1

TELECOMMUNICATIONS
Distance, speed and time — 2
Speed of light — 3
Echo problems — 3
Wave definitions — 4
Wave equations — 5
Mixed problems — 6
Radio and television — 7
Reflection and diffraction — 9
Satellites — 11

USING ELECTRICITY
Charge and current — 12
Circuit symbols — 13
Circuits — 14
Ohm's law — 16
Power and energy — 17
Power, current and voltage — 18
Power, current and resistance — 19
Power, voltage and resistance — 20
Mixed problems on power — 21
Series and parallel circuits — 23
Resistors in series and parallel — 24
Circuits — 27
Fuses — 29
Cost of electricity — 30
Movement from electricity — 32

HEALTH PHYSICS
Thermometers — 34
Sound — 35
Light — 37
Power of a lens — 38
Fibre optics — 39
Lasers — 39
Using the spectrum — 40
Nuclear medicine — 41
Half life — 42

ELECTRONICS
Output devices — 44
Protective resistors — 44
Voltage dividers — 46
Thermistors and Ldrs — 47
Capacitors — 49
Switching circuits — 50
Logic gates — 52
Clock pulse generators — 55
Analogue processes — 56

Voltage gain	**56**
Power, voltage and resistance	**57**
Power gain	**57**
Mixed problems on amplifiers	**58**

TRANSPORT

Average and instantaneous speed	**59**
Acceleration	**61**
Speed time graphs	**62**
Weight	**64**
Newton's First Law	**65**
Resultant force	**66**
Newton's Second Law	**66**
Work done	**70**
Potential energy	**71**
Kinetic energy	**72**
Energy and power	**73**
Potential and kinetic energy	**74**
General problems	**75**

ENERGY MATTERS

Sources of energy	**78**
Power stations	**79**
Efficiency	**80**
Energy conversions	**82**
Transformers	**84**
Current in transformers	**86**
Complete transformer equation	**87**
Efficiency in transformers	**88**
Transmission lines	**89**
Heat energy	**90**
Heat	**93**
Temperature - time graphs	**95**
Mixed problems on heat	**96**

SPACE PHYSICS

Distances in space	**97**
Telescopes	**98**
Ray diagrams	**99**
Visible spectrum	**100**
Electromagnetic spectrum	**101**
Newton's Third Law	**102**
Gravitational field strength	**103**
Projectiles	**104**
Rockets and space craft	**106**

GRAPHS **109**
FORMULAE **112**
ANSWERS **115**

Note : *The questions in italic are considered to be more demanding.*

ii

Numerical Questions for

BASIC MATHEMATICS

SCIENTIFIC NOTATION   (e.g. 3×10^8)

1. Write the following in scientific notation:
   a) 370 000 000
   b) 20 050 000 000
   c) 930 000 000 000 000
   d) 0.000 23
   e) 0.000 000 06
   f) 0.000 000 000 04

2. Write out the following in full:
   a) 3×10^8
   b) 2.75×10^4
   c) 7.004×10^9
   d) 8.4×10^{-3}
   e) 4.2×10^{-8}
   f) 9.08×10^{-5}

PREFIXES   (e.g. k, M, m, µ, n)

3. Convert the following to volts:
   a) 5 kV
   b) 23 mV
   c) 7 µV
   d) 2.8 MV
   e) 67 nV
   f) 389 µV

4. Use the correct prefix to write the following in the shortest possible form:
   a) 8 000 000 J
   b) 0.000 004 J
   c) 6340 J
   d) 0.005 J
   e) 0.000 063 J
   f) 9 806 000 J

BASIC UNITS   (e.g. m, s, kg, A, V, J)

Change the following to basic units:

5. a) 50 km
   b) 30 000 km
   c) 57 mm
   d) 9 cm
   e) 8.31 km
   f) 25 km 356 m 28 cm

6. a) 5 min
   b) 3 h
   c) 2 min 40 s
   d) 8 min 22 s
   e) 7.45 min
   f) 7 h 25 min 30 s

7. a) 500 g
   b) 7 400 000 g
   c) 250 mg
   d) 97.5 g
   e) 45 µg
   f) 3700 Mg

8. a) 800 mA
   b) 0.25 MA
   c) 375 kA
   d) 35.6 µA
   e) 35.6 kA
   f) 9 430 000 µA

9. a) 750 mV
   b) 4.7 MV
   c) 450 kV
   d) 53 µV
   e) 281 kV
   f) 10 670 000 µV

10. a) 56 kJ
    b) 78 mJ
    c) 8000 MJ
    d) 0.3 µJ
    e) 0.0075 MJ
    f) 3600 µJ

SIGNIFICANT FIGURES

11. Write the following numbers correct to three significant figures:
    a) 54.293
    b) 1239.24
    c) 29.650 01
    d) 3 259 452
    e) 0.855 41
    f) 2 575 000

TELECOMMUNICATIONS

DISTANCE, SPEED AND TIME $d = v t$

1. Complete the following table:

	SPEED	TIME	DISTANCE
a)	20 m s^{-1}	5 s	----------
b)	----------	6 s	36 m
c)	5 m s^{-1}	----------	40 m
d)	----------	3 min	720 m
e)	25 m s^{-1}	----------	3.5 km
f)	75 cm s^{-1}	2 min 30 s	----------
g)	----------	1 h	43.2 km

2. Sound travels at 340 m s^{-1}. How far does it travel in 5 s?

3. A girl standing 1330 m away from a lightning strike hears the thunder 4 s after she sees the lightning. What is the speed of sound?

4. If sound travels at 333 m s^{-1}, how long does it take to travel 3000 m?

5. The sound from an explosion reaches an observer 8 s after he sees the blast.
   a) How far away is the explosion if the speed of sound is 340 m s^{-1}?
   b) What assumption are you making in the above calculation?

6. A diver 4.5 km away from a diving bell hears the hooter to return 3 s after it is sounded. What value does this give for the speed of sound in water?

7. If the speed of sound in water is 1500 m s^{-1}, how far does it travel in 3 min 45 s?

8. Sound travels at 5050 m s^{-1} in railway tracks. A train is 4 km away. How long does the sound take to reach a man with his ear to the tracks?

9. Sound takes 3×10^{-3} s to travel through a copper bar which is 10.5 m long. What value does this give for the speed of sound in copper?

SPEED OF LIGHT   ($c = 3 \times 10^8$ m s^{-1})

10. Calculate the distance that light travels in:
    a) 10 s,
    b) 5 min.

11. A boy hears the thunder 4 s after he sees the lightning.
    a) How far from the boy is the lightning strike?
    b) How long does it take the light to travel this distance?

12. Microwaves travel at the same speed as light. How long does the signal take to travel down a microwave link of 450 km between Inverness and Stranraer?

13. Radio waves travel at the same speed as light. A radio signal is sent 50 000 km up to a satellite from Edinburgh and has to travel the same distance down from the satellite to the receiving station in Washington. How long will it take to send a message and receive an answer (assume no delay in sending the answer)?

14. Twins, Carol and Peter, both want to hear a concert. Peter is at the open air arena but he is 250 m from the stage. Carol is 15 000 km away in South America. Carol has to listen on the radio but Peter hears the sound directly from the loudspeakers.
    a) How long does the sound take to reach Peter?
    b) How long does the radio wave take to reach Carol?
    c) Which of them hears the start of the concert first?

ECHO PROBLEMS

15. A boy is standing in front of a canyon wall. He shouts and hears the echo 0.24 s later. Take the speed of sound to be 340 m s^{-1}.
    a) Calculate the total distance which is travelled by the sound.
    b) How far from the wall is the boy standing?

16. Sonar consists of sound waves which reflect from the sea bed or objects under the sea. A sonar pulse was sent down from a ship looking for a shoal of fish and two pulses were reflected back, the first after 0.85 s and the second after 2.3 s.
    Take the speed of sound in water to be 1500 m s^{-1}.
    a) Calculate the depth of the water.
    b) Calculate the depth at which the fish are swimming.

17. A girl standing in front of a tall building claps her hands four times every second. She hears the echo of one clap just as she makes the next one.
    If the speed of sound is 340 m s^{-1}, how far is she from the building?

18. A man shouts and hears the echo from a cliff 4 s later. Then he walks towards the cliff and tries again. This time he hears the echo after 2.5 s
    If the speed of sound is 340 m s^{-1}, how far has he walked?

WAVE DEFINITIONS

19.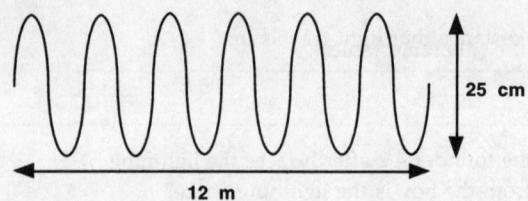
    a) What is the amplitude of the wave shown?
    b) What is the wavelength of the wave?

20. 20 waves pass a point in 4 s.
    a) What is the frequency of the waves?
    b) What is the period of the waves?

21.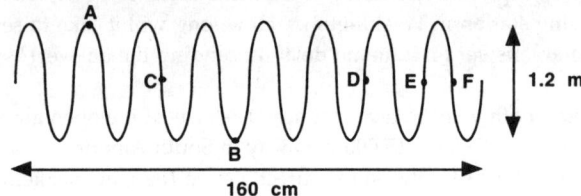

    All the waves shown were produced in 2 s.
    a) Calculate the frequency of the waves.
    b) Calculate the wavelength of the waves.
    c) Calculate the period of the waves.
    d) Calculate the amplitude of the waves.
    e) Name the points: i) A , ii) B.
    f) Calculate the distance separating the points: i) C and D, ii) E and F.

22. The circles shown represent wave fronts. The distance X is 50 m and the waves are produced in 10 s.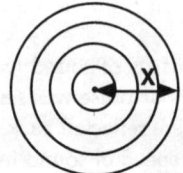
    a) Calculate the wavelength of the wave.
    b) Calculate the frequency of the waves.
    c) Calculate the period of the waves.
    d) Calculate the speed of the waves.

23. A generator producing waves vibrates 480 times every minute.
    a) What is the frequency of the waves?
    b) What is the period of the waves?

24. A boat is anchored in a bay and 10 waves pass it every minute. The average distance between the crests of the waves is 15 m.
    a) What is the frequency of the waves?
    b) What is the wavelength of the waves?
    c) What is the speed of the waves?

WAVE EQUATION $v = f\lambda$, $f = \dfrac{1}{T}$

25. Complete the following table:

	WAVELENGTH	FREQUENCY	PERIOD	SPEED
a)	7 m	8 Hz	----i)----	----ii)----
b)	----i)----	----ii)----	0.25 s	36 m s^{-1}
c)	5 cm	----i)----	----ii)----	60 m s^{-1}
d)	----i)----	----ii)----	62.5 μs	320 m s^{-1}
e)	15 m	20 MHz	----i)----	----ii)----
f)	95 mm	----i)----	----ii)----	7.6 m s^{-1}
g)	----i)---	375 kHz	----ii)----	87.5 cm s^{-1}

26. A wave has a wavelength of 34 cm and a frequency of 75 Hz. Calculate its speed.

27. A wave travelling at 25 m s^{-1} has a wavelength of 7.5 mm. Calculate its frequency.

28. A wave has a velocity of 18 m s^{-1} and a frequency of 9 Hz.
   a) Calculate the wavelength of the wave.
   b) Calculate the period of the wave.

29. A light wave has a wavelength of 5×10^{-7} m. Calculate its frequency.

30. What is the wavelength of a microwave which has a frequency of 12 500 MHz?

31. Radio 1 has a wavelength of 285 m. What is its frequency?

32. Radio Clyde transmits at a frequency of 2927 kHz. Calculate its wavelength?

33. 96 waves arrive at a beach every minute. The speed of the waves is 4.8 m s^{-1}.
   a) Calculate the frequency of the waves.
   b) Calculate the wavelength of the waves.

34. A source produces 400 waves every minute. If the speed of the waves is 8 mm s^{-1}, find the distance between adjacent crests?

Standard Grade Physics

MIXED PROBLEMS $d = vt$, $v = f\lambda$, $f = \dfrac{1}{T}$

35. A wave has a wavelength of 12 m and a frequency of 6 Hz.
    a) Calculate the wave speed.
    b) How far does the wave travel in 1 min?

36. 256 waves pass a point in 32 s. They have a wavelength of 5 cm.
    a) Calculate the frequency and the period of the wave.
    b) Calculate the wave speed.
    c) How long does it take the waves to travel 48 m?

37. 1080 waves pass a point in 1 min and their wavelength is 15 cm.
    a) What is the wave speed in metres per second?
    b) What distance will the waves travel in 5 min?

38. A wave travels 60 m in 30 s. It has a wavelength of 5 cm.
    a) Calculate the wave speed.
    b) Calculate the frequency of the wave.
    c) Calculate the period of the wave.

39. A wave travels 360 km in 4 min. It has a period of 7.5×10^{-4} s.
    a) Calculate the wave speed.
    b) Calculate the frequency of the wave.
    c) Calculate the wavelength.

40. A wave travels 12 km in 3 min and it has a wavelength of 25 cm.
    a) Calculate the wave speed.
    b) Calculate the frequency of the wave.
    c) Calculate the period of the wave.

41. A wave has a wavelength of 50 cm and a frequency of 2 kHz.
    How long does it take the wave to travel a distance of 4 km?

42. A wave has a frequency of 25 kHz and a wavelength of 400 μm.
    What distance does it travel in 14 min?

43. 1500 waves pass a point in 1 min with a wavelength of 6 cm.
    a) Calculate the wave speed.
    b) Calculate how far the wave travels in 3.25 min.

44. A pulse of light has a wavelength of 7×10^{-7} m. It travels through diamond for 8.2×10^{-12} s at a speed of 1.25×10^{8} m s^{-1}.
    a) Calculate the distance travelled by the light in the diamond.
    b) Calculate the frequency of the light.
    c) Calculate the distance the light would have travelled in air in the same time.

45. Show that $v = f\lambda$ and $v = \dfrac{d}{t}$ are equivalent.

RADIO AND TELEVISION

46. a) Name parts i) to iv) in the block diagram for a radio receiver.

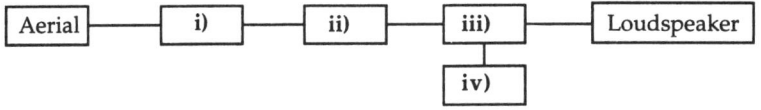

47. Which parts in a radio receiver do the following diagrams represent?

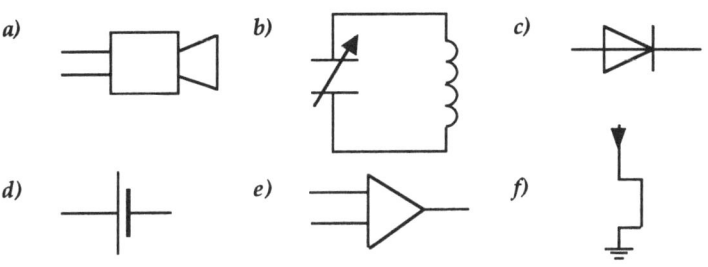

a)   b)   c)   d)   e)   f)

48. a) What is meant by modulation?
    b) Draw the wave that would be produced when the audio wave shown is added to a carrier wave:
       i) to give an amplitude modulated wave,
       ii) to give a frequency modulated wave.

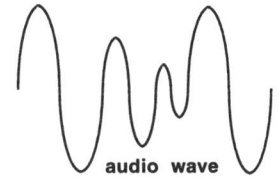

audio wave

49. How far does a radio wave travel in 1 min?

50. How long does it take a radio wave to travel from London to Edinburgh, a distance of 665 km?

51. The markings below are seen on the dial of a radio receiver.

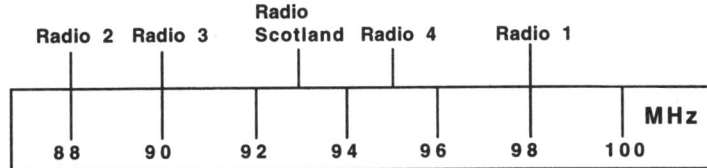

   a) Draw a table to show the frequencies of the radio stations.
   b) Calculate the wavelength of Radio Scotland.
   c) What control would you adjust on your radio to change station?
   d) Classic F.M. has a wavelength of 2.97 m. What frequency does it have?

52. Describe how a moving television picture is formed. Include: where the light energy comes from, the production of one picture, the number of pictures every second, changes between them and remanence of vision.

Standard Grade Physics

53. What are the three primary colours for light?

54. State the colour which is obtained when the following beams of equally bright light overlap on a white screen:
    a) red and blue
    b) blue and green
    c) red and green
    d) cyan and red
    e) yellow and blue
    f) red, green and blue

55. Draw the block diagram for a television receiver, equivalent to the one for the radio receiver in **Q.45**.

56. In a television receiver there are 625 lines making each picture and 25 pictures are produced every second.
    a) How many pictures are produced in 1 min?
    b) How many lines are drawn in 1 min?
    c) A man dozes off for 5 min. How many pictures does he miss?

57. a) If there are 25 pictures produced in 1 s on a television receiver, how long does it take to produce 1 picture?
    b) If the picture consists of 625 lines, how long does it take to produce 1 line?
    c) If the line is 45 cm long, how fast is the electron beam travelling across the screen?

58. a) BBC1 uses 623 to 631 MHz for transmission.
       To what wavelength range does this correspond?
    b) Why does television need such a wide range for one channel?

59. A television station uses 0.371 m to 0.375 m for transmission.
    a) What frequency range does this correspond to?
    b) If the signal has to travel 120 km from the transmitter to the receiver, how long does this take?

60. A taxi firm in Glasgow uses radio to keep in touch with the cabs. One cab uses a frequency of 180 MHz and the main office transmits at 188 MHz.
    a) Why do the cab and the main office use different frequencies?
    b) To what wavelength must the main office tune its receiver in order to get messages from the cab?
    c) In order to receive radio messages inside the cab, a receiver and one other piece of equipment are needed.
       i) What is the name of the other piece of equipment?
       ii) Why is it needed?
    d) A second firm in Edinburgh also uses 188 MHz.
       Why does this not cause problems?

REFLECTION AND DIFFRACTION

61. a) What term is given to the bending of waves round an obstacle?
b) Which bend more, waves with short or long wavelengths?

62. Copy and complete the following diagrams for waves moving towards the barriers:
a) 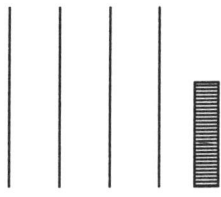 b)

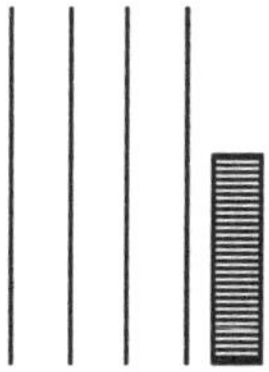

c) 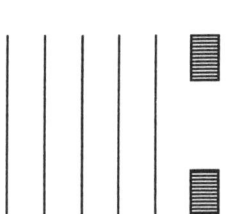 d)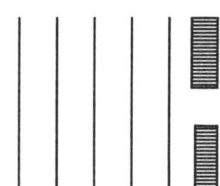

63. Which property of light allows you to see yourself in a mirror?

64. Copy and complete the following diagrams for light rays meeting mirrors:

a) 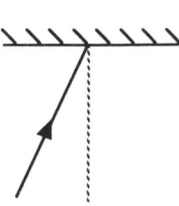 b) 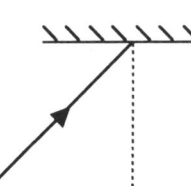 c)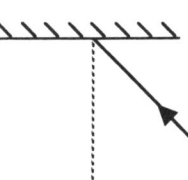

d) 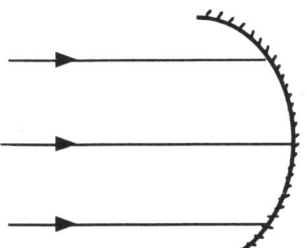 e)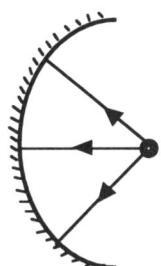

Standard Grade Physics

65. Explain what is meant by 'total internal reflection'.

66. Copy and complete the following diagrams:

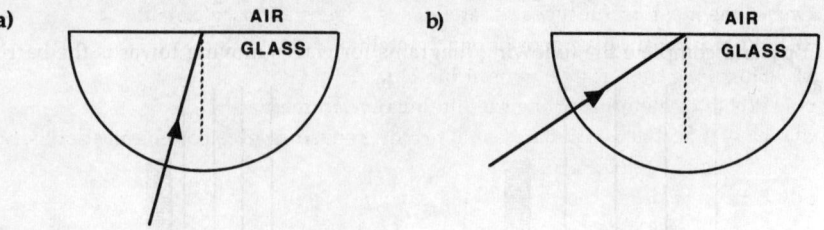

   c) What is happening in diagram (b)?
   d) What is the name of the smallest angle at which this occurs?

67. Draw a diagram to show how light passes along an optical fibre.

68. Light travels through an optical fibre at 2×10^8 m s^{-1}. A live transmission is sent from Los Angeles to Edinburgh via an optical fibre link. It has to travel a total distance of 10 000 km. How long does the signal take to arrive?

69. Copy and complete the following diagrams:

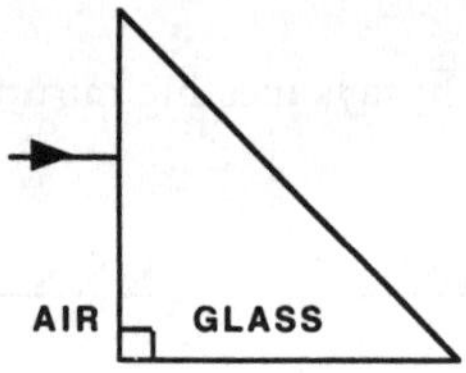

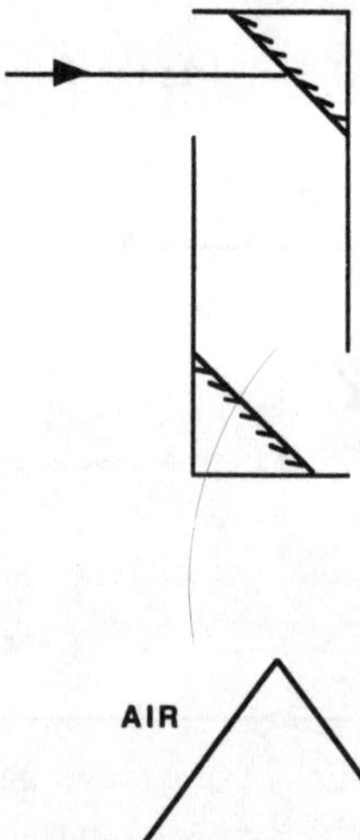

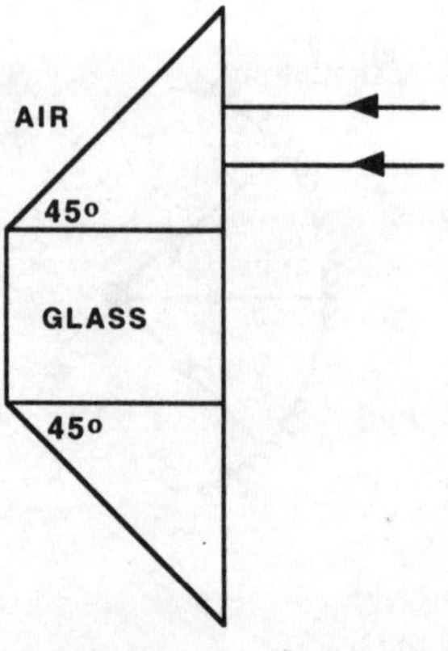

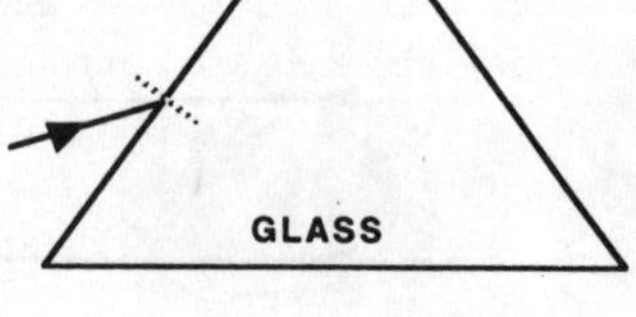

SATELLITES

70. What determines the period of a satellite?

71. One of the most useful types of satellites is a 'geostationary' satellite.
    a) What is meant by a geostationary satellite?
    b) How long does it take to orbit the Earth?
    c) Where is the orbit of the satellite relative to the Earth?
    d) How many geostationary satellites are needed to give communication between all points on the Earth?
    e) How high above the earth is the satellite placed?

72. Suggest possible periods for satellites orbiting at:
    a) 10 000 km,
    b) 36 000 km,
    c) 50 000 km.

73. Explain why a curved reflector is needed:
    a) at the aerial transmitting signals to a satellite,
    b) at the aerial receiving signals from a satellite.

74. A satellite receives information from a ground station at 5.2 GHz and transmits information to the Earth at 5.6 GHz (1 GHz = 1×10^9 Hz).
    a) Why are two frequencies used?
    b) Calculate the two wavelengths which are used.
    c) What else is done to the signal at the satellite apart from the change of frequency?

75. One of the first communications satellites was 'Early Bird'. When it was used to send television pictures from USA to Britain, the pictures could only be received for 20 min in each 90 min.
    a) What was the period of the satellite?
    b) Why were pictures only received for 20 min?
    c) The signal had to travel 80 000 km from the USA to Britain via Early Bird. Calculate how long this took.
    d) If the wavelength of one signal was 15 cm, calculate its frequency.

76. Telephone signals are sent down links using optical fibres, microwaves or copper cable. Each type of link needs repeater stations. These are placed 100 km apart for optical fibres, 40 km apart for microwaves and 4 km apart for copper cable.
    a) How many repeater stations are required with copper cable if the signal has to travel 72 000 m?
    b) How many repeater stations are required with microwaves if the signal has to travel 1200 km?
    c) How many repeater stations are required with optical fibres for a signal travelling 5×10^5 m?
    d) How many extra repeater stations are required with copper cable instead of optical fibres if the signal has to travel 13 400 km?

USING ELECTRICITY

CHARGE AND CURRENT   Q = I t

1. Complete the following table:

	CHARGE	TIME	CURRENT
a)	200 C	40 s	--------
b)	-------	15 s	4 A
c)	900 C	------	5 A
d)	-------	3 min	7.5 mA
e)	160 mC	0.04 s	-------
f)	900 mC	------	4.5 µA
g)	648 kC	24 h	-------

2. How many types of charge are there?

3. State what happens when:
   a) two positive charges are brought close together,
   b) two negative charges are brought close together,
   c) a positive and negative charge are brought close together.

4. A lightning strike lasts for 2.8 ms and delivers 50.4 C of charge. Calculate the current during the lightning strike.

5. How much charge flows along a wire when 25 µA passes for 2 h?

6. If a capacitor stores 20 mC of charge, how long does it take to discharge, if the average discharge current is 0.4 µA?

7. If 72 kC of charge flows through a resistor in 4 h, calculate the current?

8. How much charge is transported if a current of 3 mA passes for 6 min?

9. In a television set there is a current of 2.8 A drawn from the plug and a current of 75 mA passing along the tube to the screen.
   a) How much charge is delivered to the set in 5 min?
   b) How much charge is delivered to the screen in 5 min?
   c) If each electron has a charge of 1.6×10^{-19} C, how many electrons are delivered to the screen in 5 min?

CIRCUIT SYMBOLS

10. Complete the following table:

	NAME	SYMBOL
a)	----------	—|⊢
b)	Battery	----------
c)	----------	—[ ]—
d)	----------	—⊗—
e)	Fuse	----------
f)	----------	—|⊢
g)	Diode	----------
h)	Variable Resistor	----------

11. Draw the circuit diagrams for the following circuits:
    a) a battery connected in series to two bulbs, a resistor and a switch
    b) an a.c. supply connected in series to a lamp, a variable resistor and a capacitor

12. Draw the circuit diagrams for the following circuits:
    a) a bulb in series with a resistor connected in parallel to a second bulb in series with a switch, both bulbs powered by a battery
    b) a cell connected in parallel with a capacitor in series with a resistor and a diode also in series with a resistor

13. a) Draw the circuit diagram for the circuit which has two cells in series with a switch, a variable resistor and a parallel network which consists of bulb **A** in series with a fuse and bulb **B** in series with a capacitor.
    b) Add an ammeter to circuit a) to measure the current through bulb **A** and a voltmeter to measure the voltage across the capacitor.

14. Describe in words the following circuits:
    a) 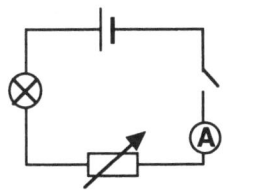 b)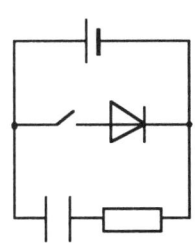

CIRCUITS

15. For the following circuits state whether the bulbs are connected in series or parallel:

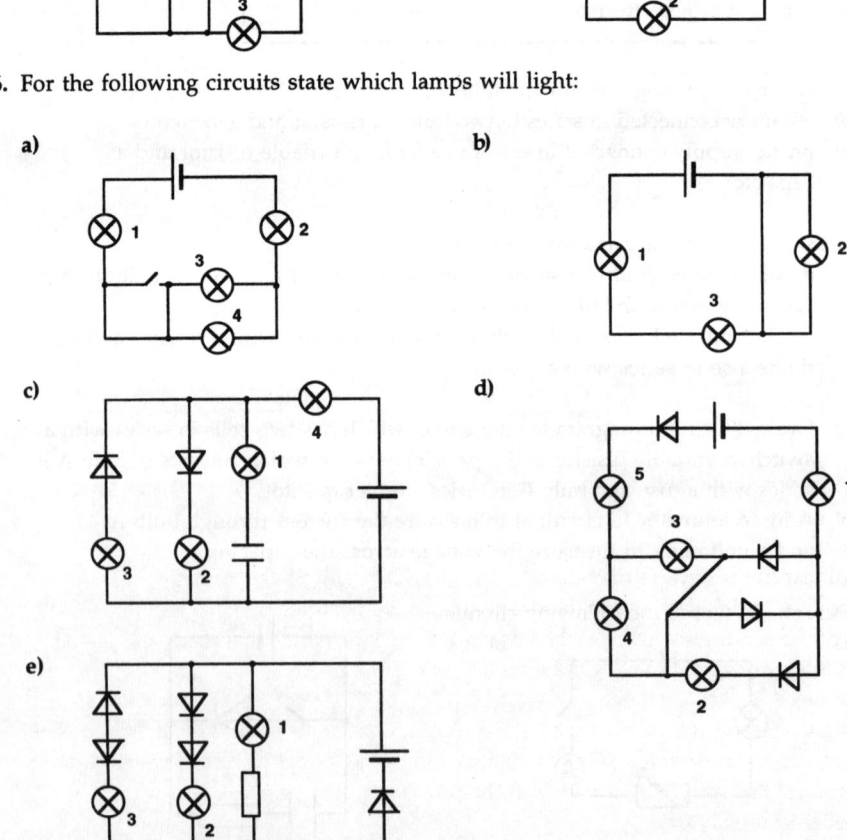

16. For the following circuits state which lamps will light:

17. Copy the following circuits and add a voltmeter to measure the voltage across the component marked X and an ammeter to measure the current through the component marked Y:

a)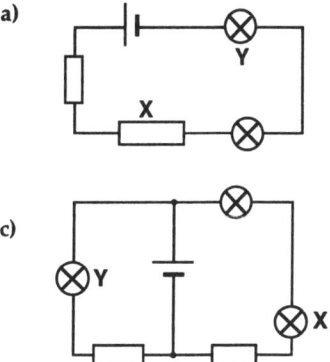
b)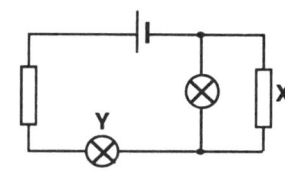

c)
d)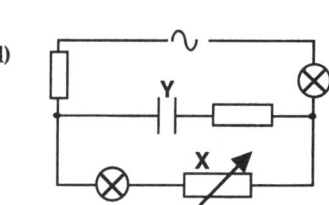

e) What type of ammeter and voltmeter must be used for the measurements in circuit **d)**?

18. In the following circuits, state which lamps light when the switch is open and when the switch is closed:

a)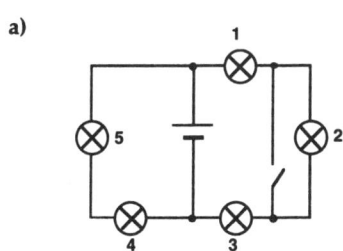
b)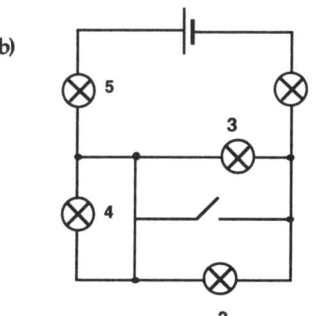

19. Draw a circuit which allows a courtesy light inside a car to be turned on when either the passenger's door or the driver's door is opened.

20. All car lights have to operate at 12 V. Draw a circuit which allows:
the four sidelights to be turned on without the headlights,
the two headlights to be turned on only if the sidelights are already on,
nothing to happen unless the ignition switch is also on.

21. Draw a circuit which allows a central heating system to be turned on from either upstairs or downstairs. The circuit also allows the boiler to be switched on to produce hot water on its own, but the pump can only be turned on when the boiler is already on.

Standard Grade Physics

OHM'S LAW $V = IR$

22. Complete the following table:

	VOLTAGE	CURRENT	RESISTANCE
a)	40 V	5 A	----------
b)	-----	2.5 A	33 Ω
c)	250 V	-------	50 Ω
d)	-----	3 mA	7 MΩ
e)	1.2 kV	0.04 mA	----------
f)	10^6 V	------	50 kΩ
g)	240 V	3×10^{-5} A	---------

23. What is the current through a 5.6 kΩ resistor when it is connected to a 240 V supply?

24. What voltage is required to produce 10.9 A of current through a 3.3×10^4 Ω resistor?

25. If a 12 V supply produces a current of 15 µA through a resistor, calculate the resistance.

26. A variable resistor can be adjusted from 10 Ω to 10 kΩ, and is connected to a mains supply.
    a) Calculate the maximum current.
    b) Calculate the minimum current.

27. A 9 V battery is connected to a variable resistor and an ammeter. The reading on the ammeter varies from 100 µA to 50 mA as the resistor is adjusted. Calculate the range of the variable resistor.

28. Three resistors of 3.3 Ω, 12 Ω and 27 Ω are connected in parallel to a 9 V battery. Hence, each resistor has 9 V across it.
    a) Calculate the current through each resistor.
    b) Calculate the total current which the battery has to provide.

29. Three resistors of 8.3 Ω, 10 Ω and 15 Ω are connected in series with a battery and a current of 150 mA passes through them.
    a) Calculate the voltage across each resistor.
    b) What is the voltage of the battery?

POWER AND ENERGY $\quad E = Pt$

30. Complete the following table:

	POWER	TIME	ENERGY
a)	100 W	5 s	----------
b)	-----	750 s	5×10^4 J
c)	25 mW	-----	5 J
d)	-----	3 ms	7 µJ
e)	1.2 kW	5 min	----------
f)	50 W	-----	10^6 kJ
g)	-----	0.5 h	6.9×10^5 J

31. A capacitor stores 40 mJ and is discharged in 0.03 s. What power does it develop?

32. How much energy, in joules, is dissipated in 1 h by a 3 kW electric fire?

33. How long does it take to completely discharge a battery which stores 2×10^3 MJ and is used to power a 6 kW heater?

34. A 20 mW LED is run from a small battery which stores 50 kJ of energy. How long does it take the LED to use up all this energy?

35. A 12 V power supply is connected to an immersion heater. If it is used for 2.5 min and provides 9 kJ of energy, what is the power of the immersion heater?

36. How much energy, in joules, is used when three 100 W bulbs, an electric fire with two bars each 2 kW and a 600 W television are used for 6 h?

37. In general, which type of devices have the highest power ratings?

38. Suggest possible power ratings for the following mains appliances:
    a) a colour television set
    b) a light bulb
    c) an electric fire
    d) a kettle
    e) a cooker with 4 rings, a grill and an oven
    f) a hair dryer

Standard Grade Physics

POWER, CURRENT AND VOLTAGE $P = IV$

39. Complete the following table:

	CURRENT	VOLTAGE	POWER
a)	2 A	----------	12 W
b)	----------	240 V	3×10^3 W
c)	25 mA	250 mV	----------
d)	----------	800 V	4×10^2 W
e)	7 μA	----------	0.00021 W
f)	3.2 mA	5 kV	----------
g)	---------	240 V	6.9×10^3 W

40. Calculate the power consumption of the following devices:
    a) a 2 V LED drawing 10 mA
    b) a mains lamp drawing 250 mA
    c) an electric kettle working from the mains taking 12.5 A
    d) a mains television set which takes 2.75 A

41. Calculate the current through the following devices:
    a) a mains heater rated at 2 kW
    b) a 250 W hair dryer which works from a 36 V battery
    c) an electric train with a power of 6 W running from a 12 V battery
    d) a transistor requiring 5 V and dissipating a power of 0.2 mW

42. Calculate the voltage required to run the following at their rated power level:
    a) a 1500 kW generator carrying 30 A
    b) a 5 mW diode carrying 0.00125 A
    c) a hair-dryer rated at 550 W carrying 4.6 A
    d) an immersion heater rated at 2.4 kW carrying 10 A

43. A 100 Ω resistor carries a current of 2 A.
    a) Calculate the voltage across the resistor.
    b) Calculate the power dissipated in the resistor.

44. 400 kV is applied to a 50 MΩ resistor.
    a) Calculate the current in the resistor.
    b) Calculate the power dissipated in the resistor.

45. Show that $P = IV$ and $P = I^2R$ are equivalent.

POWER, CURRENT AND RESISTANCE $P = I^2 R$

46. Complete the following table:

	POWER	CURRENT	RESISTANCE
a)	40 W	--------	10 Ω
b)	-------	0.03 A	2×10^3 Ω
c)	100 W	5 A	--------
d)	-------	8 mA	4×10^5 Ω
e)	5760 W	--------	10^3 Ω
f)	6 mW	5 μA	--------
g)	-------	7 mA	1 MΩ

47. Calculate the power which is dissipated in the following resistors:
    a) a 1 kΩ resistor carrying 50 mA
    b) a 5 MΩ resistor carrying 2.5 mA
    c) a 680 Ω resistor carrying 3×10^{-2} A
    d) a 390 Ω resistor carrying 27 mA

48. Calculate the resistance of the resistor when:
    a) a rated power of 500 W requires a current of 0.05 A,
    b) a rated power of 4.5 kW requires a current of 300 mA,
    c) a rated power of 10 mW requires a current of 250 μA,
    d) a rated power of 5 MW requires a current of 2×10^2 A.

49. Calculate the current in the following resistors when used at their maximum power rating:
    a) a 0.5 Ω resistor, rated at 4.5 W
    b) a 1 kΩ resistor, rated at 640 W
    c) a 75 Ω resistor, rated at 3 kW
    d) a 3×10^4 Ω resistor, rated at 7200 W

50. In 1 min a charge of 120 C flows through a resistor which dissipates 25 W.
    a) Calculate the current which passes.
    b) Calculate the resistance of the resistor.

51. There is a voltage of 12 V across a 3 kΩ resistor.
    a) Calculate the current in the resistor.
    b) What power must the resistor dissipate?

Standard Grade Physics

POWER, VOLTAGE AND RESISTANCE $P = \frac{V^2}{R}$

52. Complete the following table:

	POWER	VOLTAGE	RESISTANCE
a)	40 W	---------	10 Ω
b)	---------	500 V	2×10^3 Ω
c)	25 000 W	5 kV	---------
d)	---------	50 mV	2.5 Ω
e)	16 kW	---------	10^5 Ω
f)	640 mW	---------	1 MΩ
g)	---------	19 mV	100 mΩ

53. Calculate the power which is dissipated in the following devices:
    a) a mains heater with 2 kΩ resistance
    b) a 2 V LED with a resistance of 300 Ω
    c) a resistor of 10 kΩ connected to a 36 V battery
    d) a 25 Ω toy car motor connected to a 1.5 V cell

54. Calculate the resistance of the following devices:
    a) a mains heater rated at 5 kW
    b) a 2.4 kW heater running from a 120 volt supply
    c) a 56 W toy train operating on a 12 volt supply
    d) a 3 mW component running off a 1.5 V cell

55. Calculate the voltage which is required to operate the following devices at their full power rating:
    a) a 25 Ω, 6 W lamp
    b) a 5 kΩ, 450 mW model car
    c) a 250 Ω, 5 mW diode
    d) a 0.35 MΩ, 4×10^4 W generator

56. A bulb is rated at 20 V, 80 W.
    a) Calculate the resistance of the bulb.
    b) Calculate the current when the bulb works at its rated value.

57. A 2 kW heater has a resistance of 26.45 Ω. Calculate the voltage and the current required to operate the heater at its standard rating.

58. Show that $P = IV$ and $P = \frac{V^2}{R}$ are equivalent.

MIXED PROBLEMS ON POWER $E = Pt, P = IV, P = I^2R, P = \dfrac{V^2}{R}$

59. Complete the following table (in each case assume that the time is 10 s):

	POWER	VOLTAGE	CURRENT	RESISTANCE	ENERGY
a)	1000 W	----i)-----	-----ii)-----	10 Ω	----iii)----
b)	----i)-----	50 V	-----ii)-----	4×10^3 Ω	----iii)----
c)	----i)-----	-----ii)-----	5 mA	----iii)----	250 J
d)	----i)-----	50 mV	-----ii)-----	2.5 Ω	----iii)----
e)	----i)-----	-----ii)-----	0.24 A	10^3 Ω	----iii)----
f)	40 kW	-----i)-----	30 A	-----ii)-----	----iii)----
g)	----i)-----	10^2 V	-----ii)-----	----iii)----	12 kJ

60. Three resistors of 500 Ω, 1 kΩ and 5 kΩ are connected in parallel so that each has 42 V across it from a power supply.
    a) Calculate the current through each resistor.
    b) Calculate the power dissipated in each resistor.
    c) Calculate the total power dissipated.
    d) Calculate the total energy used in 5 min.

61. The same three resistors as in **Q. 60** are connected in series with a power supply to give a current of 5.6 mA through each.
    a) Calculate the voltage across each resistor.
    b) What is the total voltage supplied by the power supply?
    c) Calculate the power dissipated in each resistor.
    d) Calculate the total power dissipated.
    e) Calculate the total energy used in 5 min.

62. A toy train running off a 12 V battery uses 1.5×10^5 J of energy in 1 h 30 min.
    a) Calculate the power of the train.
    b) Calculate the resistance of the train.
    c) Calculate the current through the train.
    d) How much charge is transferred in the time the train is running?

63. A heater is rated at 3 kW and has a resistance of 20 Ω.
    Calculate the current and voltage required to operate the heater at its stated rating.

Standard Grade Physics

64. Twenty Christmas lamps are connected in series across the mains supply. Each lamp has a resistance of 80 Ω.
   a) If the lights have an equal share of the voltage, what is the voltage across one lamp?
   b) What is the current in each lamp?
   c) What is the power dissipated in one lamp?
   d) How much energy is transformed by the set of lamps in 1 h?

65. The resistance of a variable resistor can vary from 0 - 100 Ω and has to be set at the right value for the motor to work at its correct rating.
   a) What is the resistance of the motor?
   b) Calculate the current required by the motor.
   c) What is the voltage across the variable resistor?
   d) What resistance setting is required by the variable resistor?

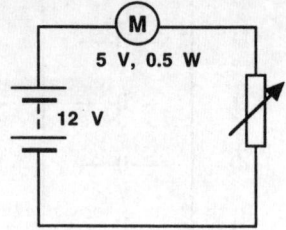

66. A fluorescent tube is rated at 240 V, 40 W.
   a) How much energy is transformed in 1 min?
   b) What forms of energy are produced?
   c) What is the advantage of a fluorescent tube over a filament lamp?

67. An electrical generator provides 9×10^7 J of energy every minute to the mains supply. It works at a voltage of 40 kV.
   a) Calculate the power of the generator.
   b) Calculate the resistance of the generator.
   c) Calculate the current through the generator.

68. A kettle has a resistance of 20 Ω and a current passing through it of 12 A.
   a) Calculate the power of the kettle.
   b) What voltage does it require?
   c) How long will it take to produce 3 MJ of energy?

69. The energy used by a mains heater in 5 min is 9×10^5 J.
   a) Calculate the power of the heater.
   b) Calculate the resistance of the heater.
   c) How much current does it draw from the mains?

70. A 75 W car vacuum cleaner runs off the 12 V car battery.
   a) What is the resistance of the vacuum cleaner?
   b) How much energy is transformed in 3.5 min?
   c) What types of energy are produced?
   d) How much charge flows through the vacuum cleaner in this time?

71. How much charge will pass through a 60 W, 960 Ω lamp in 1 min?

SERIES AND PARALLEL CIRCUITS

72. a) What can you say about the current in a series circuit?
    b) What can you say about the voltages in a series circuit?

73. a) What can you say about the current in a parallel circuit?
    b) What can you say about the voltages in a parallel circuit?

74. There is a current of 250 mA through the circuit shown.
    a) Calculate the voltage across each resistor.
    b) What is the supply voltage?
    c) Calculate the total power dissipated in the circuit.

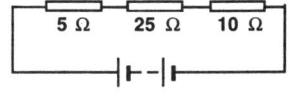

75. In the circuit shown the supply voltage is 12 V.
    a) Calculate the current in each resistor.
    b) What is the total current drawn from the battery?
    c) Calculate the total power dissipated in the circuit.

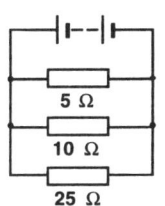

76. In the following circuits the bulbs are identical. Calculate the current through each numbered bulb:

a) 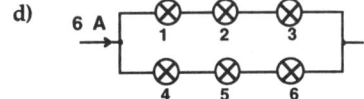   c)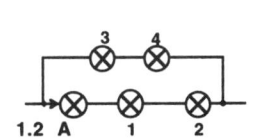

d) 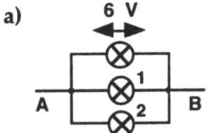   e)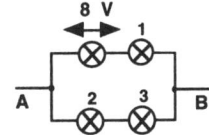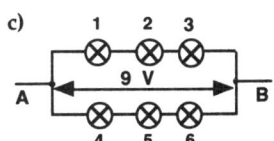

77. In the following circuits an external voltage is applied between **A** and **B** and the bulbs are identical.
    From the voltages indicated, calculate the voltage across each numbered bulb:

a)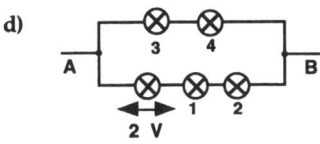

d)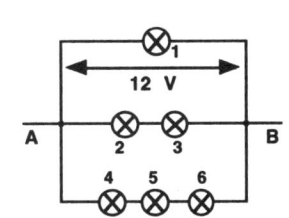

Standard Grade Physics 23

RESISTORS IN SERIES AND PARALLEL

$$R_S = R_1 + R_2, \quad \frac{1}{R_P} = \frac{1}{R_1} + \frac{1}{R_2}$$

78. Complete the following table:

	R_1	R_2	R_S	R_P
a)	10 Ω	10 Ω	----i)-----	---ii)---
b)	3 Ω	----i)-----	9 Ω	---ii)---
c)	----i)-----	100 Ω	---ii)---	50 Ω
d)	----i)-----	15 Ω	45 Ω	---ii)---
e)	5 kΩ	1250 Ω	---ii)---	---ii)---
f)	40 Ω	----i)-----	1.2×10^2 Ω	---ii)---
g)	----i)-----	12 Ω	---ii)---	4 Ω

79. The same three resistors are connected in different ways as shown. Calculate the total resistance between X and Y:

a)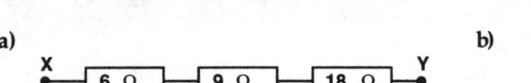

b)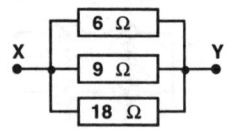

c)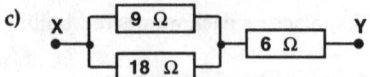

d)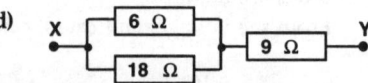

80. By considering your answers to **Q. 79 a)** and **b)**, state what can you say about:
  a) the total resistance of resistors in series compared to the largest value of resistor,
  b) the total resistance of resistors in parallel compared to the smallest value of resistor.

81. Calculate the total resistance of the circuit shown.

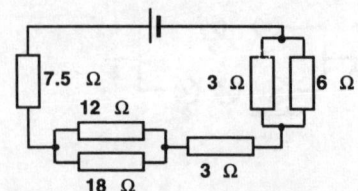

82. Calculate the total resistance between **X** and **Y** for the following networks of resistors:

a)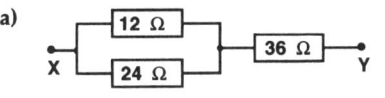

b)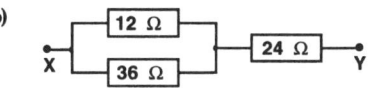

c)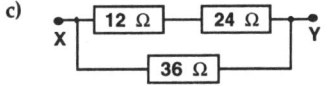

d)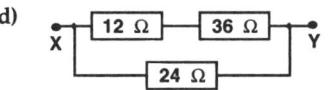

83. Calculate the total resistance between **X** and **Y** for the following networks of resistors:

a)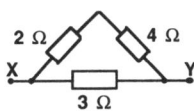

b)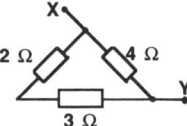

c)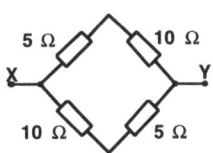

d)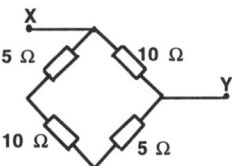

84. Calculate the total resistance between **X** and **Y** for the following networks of resistors:

a)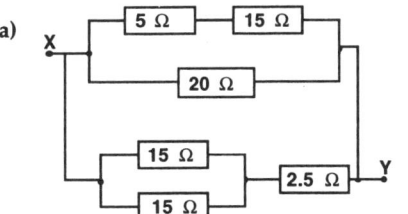

b)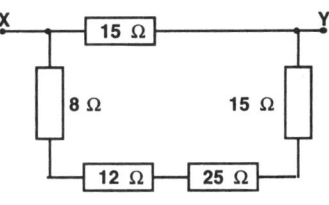

c)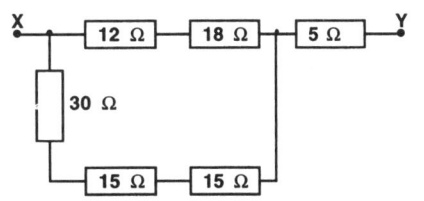

d)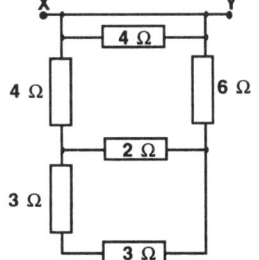

Standard Grade Physics 25

85. Calculate the total resistance between X and Y for the following network of resistors:

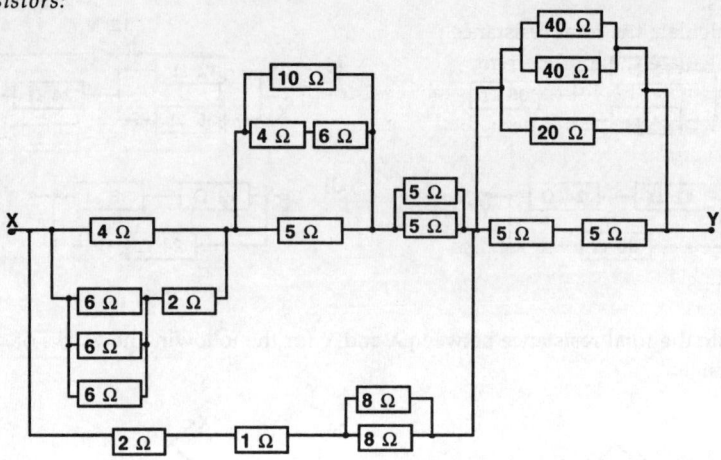

86. Calculate the total resistance between X and Y for the following network of resistors:

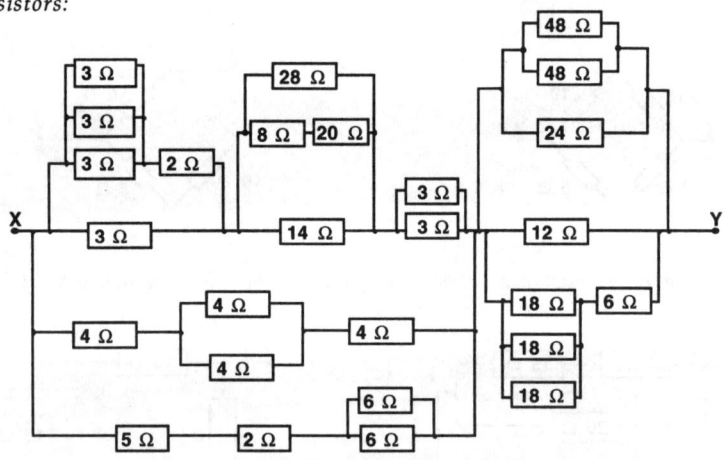

87. Calculate the total resistance between X and Y for the following network of resistors:

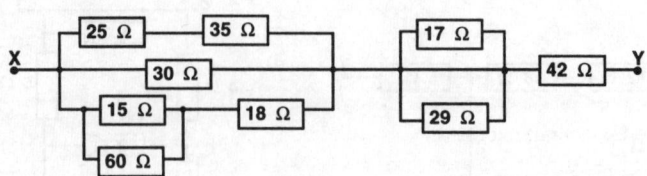

CIRCUITS

88. a) Calculate the total resistance.
    b) Calculate the total current.
    c) Calculate the voltage across each resistor.
    d) Calculate the power dissipated by each resistor.

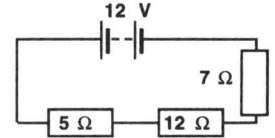

89. a) Calculate the total resistance.
    b) Calculate the total current.
    c) Calculate the voltage across each resistor.
    d) Calculate the power dissipated by each resistor.

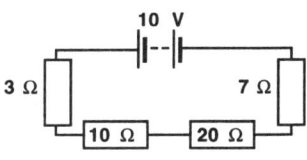

90. a) Calculate the total resistance.
    b) State the voltage across each resistor.
    c) Calculate the current through each resistor.
    d) Calculate the power dissipated by each resistor.

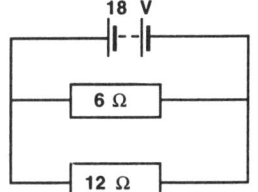

91. a) Calculate the total resistance.
    b) State the voltage across each resistor.
    c) Calculate the current through each resistor.
    d) Calculate the power dissipated by each resistor.

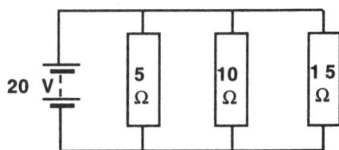

92. a) Calculate the total resistance.
    b) Calculate the total current.
    c) Calculate the voltage across the 4 Ω resistor.
    d) Calculate the voltage across the parallel network.
    e) Calculate the current for each resistor in the parallel network.
    f) Calculate the power dissipated by each resistor.

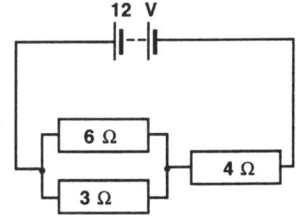

93. a) Calculate the total resistance.
    b) Calculate the total current.
    c) Calculate the voltage across the 20 Ω resistor.
    d) Calculate the voltage across the parallel network.
    e) Calculate the current for each resistor in the parallel network.
    f) Calculate the power dissipated by each resistor.

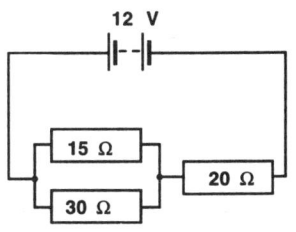

Standard Grade Physics

94. Calculate the current, voltage and power for each resistor in the following circuits:

a)

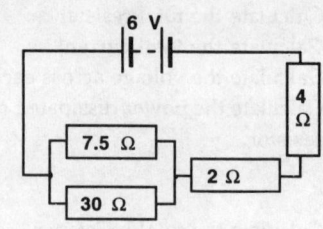

b)

95. Calculate the current, voltage and power for each resistor in the circuit opposite.

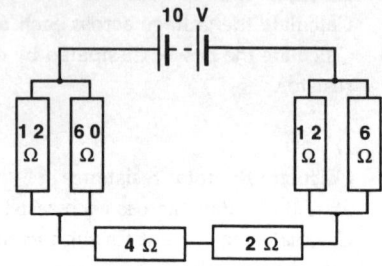

96. a) Calculate the current through bulb A.
    b) Calculate the current through bulb B.
    c) Calculate the total current in the circuit.
    d) Calculate the voltage across the resistor.
    e) Calculate the resistance of the resistor R.

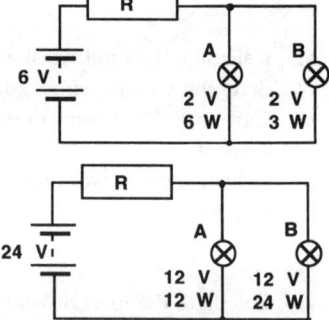

97. a) Calculate the current through bulb A.
    b) Calculate the current through bulb B.
    c) Calculate the total current in the circuit.
    d) Calculate the voltage across the resistor.
    e) Calculate the resistance of the resistor R.

98. For the following circuits, calculate the resistance of R:

a)

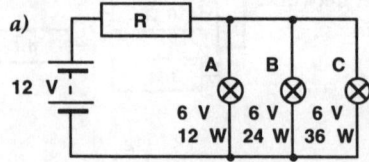

b)

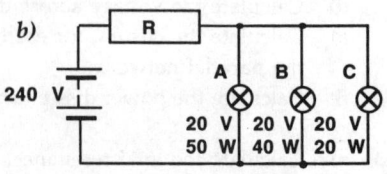

99. a) Draw a circuit, showing four lamps connected to the mains in series.
    b) Draw a circuit, showing four lamps connected to the mains in parallel.
    c) Draw a circuit, showing four lamps connected to the mains in a ring circuit.
    d) Give an advantage of circuit b) compared to circuit a)
    e) Give **two** advantages of circuit c) compared to circuit b).

100. For the following circuits, calculate the supply voltage V and the power rating of bulb X (assume that the other bulbs are working at their rated values):

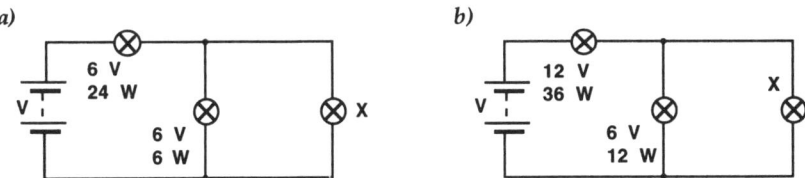

101. In the following circuit, the ammeter reads 0.5 A when the switch is open and 2 A when the switch is closed. Calculate the resistance of R_1 and R_2.

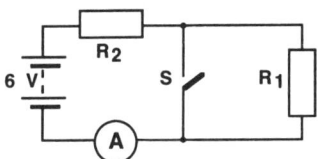

102. In the following circuit, the ammeter reads 3 A when the switch is open and 4.5 A when the switch is closed. Calculate the resistance of R_1 and R_2.

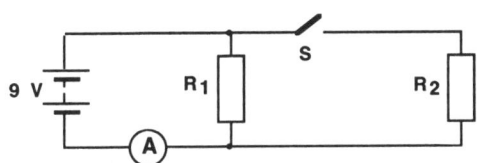

103. Three 240 V, 100 W lamps are connected in parallel to the mains.
   a) Calculate the current drawn by each individual lamp.
   b) Calculate the total current when they are connected in parallel.
   c) Estimate the current in the wires if they are connected in a ring circuit.

FUSES

104. Given the choice of a 3 A, 13 A, 15 A or 50 A fuse, state which you should choose for the following mains appliances:
   a) 100 W lamp
   b) 750 W power drill
   c) 3.5 kW immersion heater
   d) 1200 W iron
   e) 250 W television
   f) 11 kW cooker

Standard Grade Physics

105. Given the choice of a 3 A, 13 A, 15 A or 50 A fuse, state which you should choose for the following mains appliances:
   a) 350 Ω hair dryer
   b) 100 Ω television
   c) 25 Ω heater
   d) 80 Ω vacuum cleaner

106. A 600 W television, a 100 W lamp and a 2 kW heater are connected to an adaptor. Is it safe to use all three at once if the adaptor has a 13 A fuse? Explain.

107. A 2.5 kW heater and a 650 W hair dryer are connected to an adaptor. Is it is safe to use both of them at once if the adaptor has a 13 A fuse? Explain.

108. An electrical appliance requires 2.4 A and is fitted with a 3 A fuse. Explain why it would be inadvisable to use:
   a) a 1 A fuse,
   b) a 13 A fuse.

COST OF ELECTRICITY

109. Complete the following table (assume the cost of one unit is 8p):

	POWER	TIME	NUMBER OF UNITS	COST
a)	2 kW	5 h	----i)----	---ii)---
b)	3.5 kW	45 min	----i)----	---ii)---
c)	650 W	30 min	----i)----	---ii)---
d)	50 mW	7 days	----i)----	---ii)---
e)	250 W	----i)----	15	---ii)---
f)	----i)----	8 h 30 min	0.51	---ii)---
g)	500 W	----i)----	---ii)---	£1.00

110. If each unit costs 7.5 p, calculate how much it would cost to run for 5 h:
   a) two 100 W lamps,
   b) a 600 W hi-fi system,
   c) a 3.5 kW electric fire.

111. The following appliances are left on for 24 h.
   a 350 W refrigerator; a 2.5 kW electric heater; four 100 W and two 60 W lamps;
   a 500 W computer; a 1.5 kW immersion heater.
   If each unit of electricity costs 8.3 p, calculate the total cost of the electricity.

112. a) How many joules are in one kilowatt hour?
   b) Why does the Electricity Board charge for electricity in kilowatt hours rather than joules?

113. a) During the day the following appliances are used for the time shown.
   a 2 kW heater and three 100 W lamps for 8 h;
   a 3 kW kettle for 20 min;
   a 600 W television for 4.5 h.
   Calculate the total cost each day, if each unit costs 8.2 p.
   b) How many joules of energy are used by the above appliances each day?

114. A toaster has a heating element of 75 Ω resistance. It is connected to the mains supply for 100 s.
   a) How many joules of energy are used?
   b) What is the power rating of the element?
   c) How many units of electricity are used?
   d) If each unit costs 7.9 p, what is the cost of using the toaster?

115. The average daily usage of the electrical appliances in one household is:
   1 kW kettle - 0.75 h; 1.5 kW fire - 6 h; 8.5 kW cooker - 2.5 h,
   3 x 100 W lamps - 6.5 h; 800 W iron - 20 min;
   750 W television - 4.25 h and a 250 W vacuum cleaner - 15 min.
   There is a standing charge of £14 per quarter and a unit of electricity costs 7.8 p.
   Payment is made each quarter of the year (91 days).
   a) What is the total cost of units for 1 day?
   b) What is the total cost of units for the whole quarter?
   c) What payment has to be made to meet the electricity bill?

116. A car battery is rated at 12 V, 48 ampere hours. The four sidelights of the car take 0.5 A each and the two headlights take 5 A each.
   a) Explain what the car battery rating means.
   b) When all the car lights are on but nothing else, what is the current drawn from the battery?
   c) What fuse should be used on this circuit?
   d) How long will the battery last, if it was fully charged to start?
   e) How much does each kilowatt hour cost, if the car battery cost £28 when new?

Standard Grade Physics

MOVEMENT FROM ELECTRICITY

117. Consider the diagram shown. 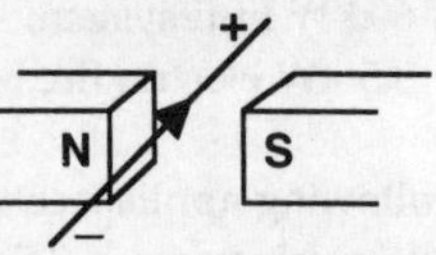
    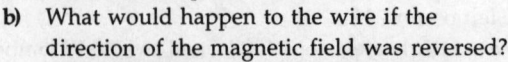
    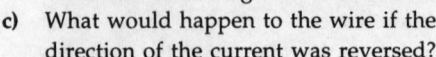
    a) What happens to the wire when current passes as shown?
    b) What would happen to the wire if the direction of the magnetic field was reversed?
    c) What would happen to the wire if the direction of the current was reversed?
    d) What would happen to the wire if both the current and the magnetic field were reversed?

118. Consider the three diagrams of a model motor shown.

    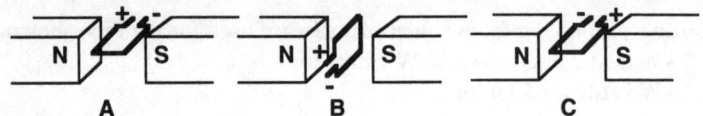

    When the current is switched on as shown in **A** the coil rotates clockwise.
    a) What happens to the coil when the current is switched on as shown in **B**?
    b) What happens to the coil when the current is switched on as shown in **C**?
    c) How is the coil connected so that it turns continuously in one direction?
    d) Give **three** changes that can be made to the above apparatus to make the coil turn faster.
    e) State **three** differences between this model motor and a commercial motor.

119. A motor has a 20 turn coil. It rotates 5 times every second when a current of 75 mA passes through it.
    a) If the coil is changed for one with 40 turns still taking 75 mA, how many rotations would there be every second?
    b) If the 20 turn coil has a current of 300 mA, what would be the maximum rate of rotation?
    c) If a coil with 60 turns is used and it draws 0.375 A, what would be the maximum rate of rotation?

120. a) When the bell push is pressed, explain what happens :
    i) to the current,
    ii) to the soft iron at **B**,
    iii) to the soft iron at **C**,
    iv) to the contact at **D**,
    v) to the current,
    vi) to the soft iron **B**,
    vii) to the contact at **D**.

    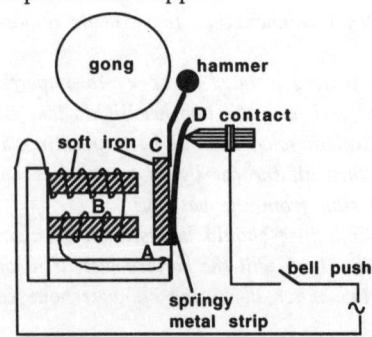

    b) What do you hear and why?

Numerical Questions for

a) What happens to the reading on the ammeter as the magnet swings in?
b) What happens to the reading on the ammeter as the magnet stops momentarily at the end of the swing?
c) What happens to the reading on the ammeter as the magnet swings back out?
d) Why is a centre zero meter required?
e) What would happen if the magnet was turned round?
f) What changes could be made to obtain a larger current?

122. A pendulum on a metal wire is swung between two magnets, with poles on their faces, as shown.
The bob swings between A and C.
There is a microammeter connected between the bob and the support, which measures a maximum current of ±40 µA.

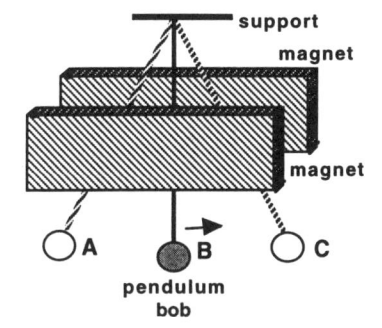

a) Why is the current a maximum when the bob is at B?
b) Why is the current zero when the bob is at C, its maximum deflection?
c) What will be the reading at B, when the bob is swinging back towards A?
d) What will be the reading at A?
e) What change could be made to increase the maximum reading at B?

Standard Grade Physics

HEALTH PHYSICS

THERMOMETERS

1. a) What is the temperature of pure boiling water?
    b) What is the temperature of melting ice?
    c) What is the normal temperature of the human body?
    d) Suggest a temperature that would indicate hypothermia.

2. All the following thermometers are identical. Thermometer **A** is in melting ice and thermometer **B** is in boiling water. The lengths of the columns of mercury are shown.

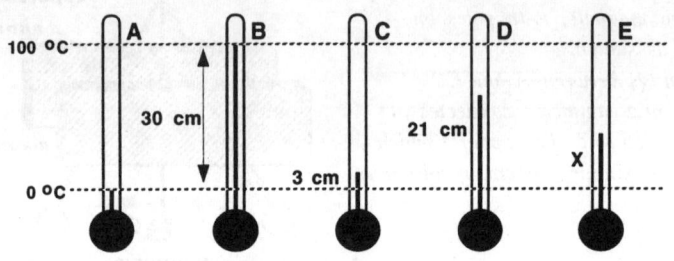

    a) What is the temperature of thermometer **C**?
    b) What is the temperature of thermometer **D**?
    c) If thermometer **E** is in water at 35 °C, what is the value of **X**?

3. A thermocouple connected to a voltmeter gives a zero reading when both junctions are in melting ice. It gives a reading of 8 mV when the second junction is in boiling water.
    a) If the second junction is in a furnace at 1200 °C, what is the voltmeter reading?
    b) If the voltmeter reads 26.8 mV, what is the temperature of the second junction?

4. a) What is a bimetallic strip?
    b) Why does a bimetallic strip bend when it is heated?
    c) A strip bends through 3.75° when it is heated by 50 °C.
       i) How much does it bend when heated by 392 °C?
       ii) What is the temperature when the strip bends through 44.1°?

5. In an alcohol in glass thermometer the column of alcohol is 215 mm from the bottom of the bulb when the thermometer is in boiling water and 45 mm from the bottom of the bulb when in melting ice.
    a) If the alcohol stops 121.5 mm from the bottom of the bulb, what is the temperature?
    b) If the alcohol stops 19.5 mm from the bottom of the bulb, what is the temperature?
    c) If the temperature is 65 °C, where does the alcohol stop?

SOUND

6. The range of human hearing is approximately 20 Hz to 20 kHz. If the speed of sound in air is 340 ms^{-1}, calculate:
   a) the minimum wavelength that is heard,
   b) the maximum wavelength that is heard.

7. The histogram shows the range of hearing for a class of pupils.

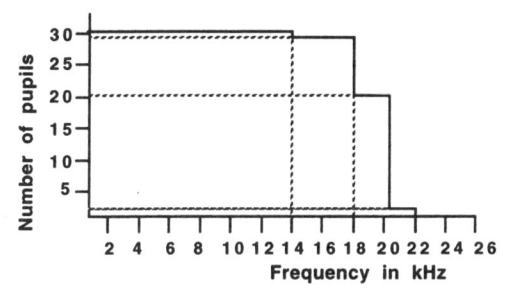

   a) What is the maximum frequency heard by any pupil?
   b) How many pupils can hear a sound of frequency 17 kHz?
   c) One pupil has a lower range than the others.
      i) What is his upper threshold of hearing?
      ii) Suggest a reason for this lower range.

8. a) State the noise level of ordinary conversation.
   b) State the pain threshold.

9. a) What is meant by ultrasound?
   b) A bat can hear sound with a wavelength of 8.5 mm. Show by calculation if this is ultrasound.

10. An object is detected by ultrasound as long as it is at least equal to one wavelength of the ultrasound. If the frequency of the ultrasound is 50 kHz, what is the size of the smallest object detected?

11. Ultrasound was applied to a pregnant woman without using a gel for good contact. The diagram shows what happened (not to scale).
    a) Name rays **B** and **C**.
    b) Calculate the size of angles **x** and **y**.

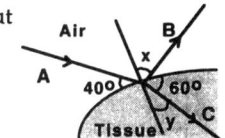

12. A series of sonar pulses is used by fishermen to detect shoals of fish under the water. The speed of sound in water is 1200 ms^{-1}.
    a) An echo is received after 0.3 s. How far had the sound travelled?
    b) How deep is the water?
    c) A second echo is received after 120 ms. How far had the sound travelled?
    d) How deep is the shoal of fish?

Standard Grade Physics

13. The speed of sound in the human body is 1500 m s^{-1} and an echo from a foetus is detected 0.1 ms after an ultrasound transmission. The frequency of the ultrasound is 250 kHz.
    a) How many pulses of ultrasound are emitted every second?
    b) What is the period of the ultrasound?
    c) How deep in the mother's body is the part of the foetus which provides the echo?

14. The speed of sound in the human body is 1500 m s^{-1} and an echo from a foetus, 5 cm inside the mother, is detected after an ultrasound transmission.
    How long does it take before the echo is received?

15. An ultrasound signal, with period of 0.45 μs and speed of 1480 m s^{-1}, is used to examine an unborn child. If an echo is received from the foetus after 0.14 ms, calculate
    a) the distance travelled and depth of the foetus inside the mother,
    b) the frequency of the wave,
    c) the wavelength of the ultrasound used.

16. An ultrasound signal, with a period of 0.8 μs and a wavelength of 1.2 mm, is used to examine an unborn child.
    a) Calculate the frequency of the ultrasound used.
    b) Calculate the speed of the ultrasound.
    c) How long will it take for an echo to be received from a depth of 6 cm?

17. An ultrasound signal, with a period of 0.75 μs and a wavelength of 1.125 mm, is used to examine an unborn child.
    a) Calculate the frequency of the ultrasound used.
    b) Calculate the speed of the ultrasound.
    c) Calculate the depth of the part of the foetus within the mother which gives an echo after:
       i) 1×10^{-4} s,
       ii) 0.1 ms,
       iii) 0.25×10^{-3} s.

18. An elephant foetus is examined at the zoo using an ultrasound with a wavelength of 1.15 mm and a period of 0.78 μs.
    a) Calculate the frequency of the ultrasound used.
    b) Calculate the speed of the ultrasound.
    c) How deep within the elephant is the part of the foetus which gives an echo after 1.2 ms?

19. A man uses a 'silent' dog whistle to call his dog.
    a) Explain why the dog can hear it but the man cannot.
    b) Suggest a possible frequency for the dog whistle.
    c) Another whistle emits sound of wavelength 18 mm.
       Will this act as a 'silent' whistle. Explain your answer.

LIGHT

20. Copy and complete the following diagrams:
    a) [diagram: incident ray in AIR hitting GLASS boundary with normal shown]
    b) [diagram: incident ray in GLASS hitting AIR boundary]

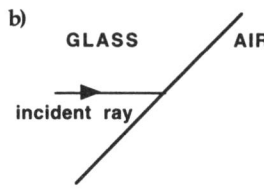

21. Copy and complete the following diagrams:
    a) [diagram: parallel rays entering a concave lens]
    b) [diagram: parallel rays entering a convex lens]

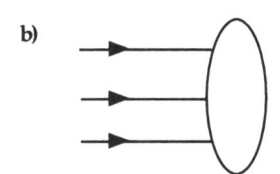

    c) Name the lenses in diagrams a) and b).

22. A convex lens has a focal length of 10 cm.
    Draw ray diagrams to scale showing the formation of the images for:
    a) an object placed 15 cm from the lens,
    b) an object placed 20 cm from the lens.

23. A convex lens has a focal length of 30 cm.
    Draw ray diagrams to scale showing the formation of the images for:
    a) an object placed 60 cm from the lens,
    b) an object placed 90 cm from the lens.

24. Describe the shape of the lens in the eye when looking at:
    a) distant objects,
    b) objects which are close by.

25. Draw diagrams to show where parallel rays of light are focused:
    a) for someone suffering from long sight,
    b) for someone suffering from short sight.

26. Describe the vision of a man suffering from:
    a) short sight,
    b) long sight.

27. A man can read his book with no trouble but needs glasses to see his cat at the bottom of the garden.
    a) What eye defect is he suffering from?
    b) What sort of lenses will be in his glasses?

Standard Grade Physics

28. A woman can watch a tennis match with no problems but needs her glasses to read the programme.
    a) What eye defect is she suffering from?
    b) What sort of lenses will be in her glasses?

29. Copy and complete the following diagrams to show the optical component which must be in the box:

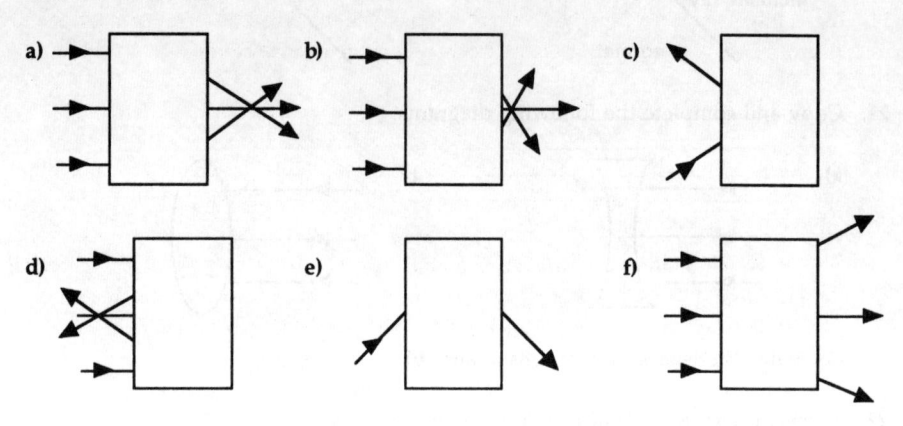

    a)   b)   c)

    d)   e)   f)

POWER OF A LENS   power of lens = $\dfrac{1}{\text{focal length in metres}}$

30. Complete the following table:

	FOCAL LENGTH	POWER	TYPE OF LENS
a)	20 cm	--------	convex
b)	----i)----	-5 D	---ii)---
c)	50 mm	----i)----	---ii)---
d)	----i)----	7.5 D	---ii)---
e)	1.2×10^{-2} m	----i)----	---ii)---
f)	----i)----	0.5 D	---ii)---
g)	- 8.5 cm	----i)----	---ii)---

31. a) A man has to wear glasses which have lenses of power 10 D.
       i) What is the focal length of the lens?
       ii) Is the man short or long sighted?
       iii) Should he wear his glasses to study a newspaper or watch football?
    b) His wife wears glasses with a focal length of -20 cm.
       i) What is the power of her lenses?
       ii) Is she short or long sighted?
       iii) When should she wear her glasses?

FIBRE OPTICS

32. Draw a diagram to show how a ray of light travels through an optical fibre.

33. Light travels along a fibre optic at 2×10^8 m s^{-1}. How long does it take a doctor to see the picture, if it has to travel 45 cm down into a patient and 45 cm back again?

34. Light travels along a fibre optic at 2×10^8 m s^{-1}. If the signal is received back 6×10^{-9} s after a pulse is sent into a patient, how long is the optical fibre?

35. a) Light can take more than one path through an optical fibre.

   i) Which of the two paths A or B will take longer to pass through the optical fibre?
   ii) What problems could this cause when using an optical fibre?
   iii) What steps could be taken to minimise this effect?
   b) Light travels down a fibre optic at 2×10^8 m s^{-1}.
   i) If it takes 4×10^{-7} s to pass along path A, how long is the fibre?
   ii) If one path is 71% shorter than the other, how long does it take to pass along path B.

LASERS

36. If a laser produces 5.8 kJ of energy in 5 min, what is its power?

37. An argon laser is used for eye surgery. It delivers 18 pulses in 0.2 s and each pulse delivers 0.023 J of energy for one particular treatment.
Calculate the power of the laser.

38. A laser has a wavelength of 610 nm and is used to destroy birthmarks. It takes 0.04 J of energy for each cm^2 of the birthmark.
   a) What is the frequency of the laser?
   b) How much energy does it require in total for a birthmark which is 16 cm^2?
   c) If the laser has a power of 2000 mW, how long will the treatment take?

39. A laser is used with an endoscope to seal an ulcer in the stomach.
If the laser has to travel 60 cm along the fibre optic to reach the ulcer and travels at 2×10^8 m s^{-1}, how long does it take?

USING THE SPECTRUM

40. Ultraviolet with wavelengths in the range 315 - 400 nm is called UVA and in the range 280 - 315 nm is called UVB.
    a) Calculate the range of frequencies which correspond to UVA.
    b) Calculate the range of frequencies which correspond to UVB.
    c) Does radiation of frequency 10^{15} Hz fall in the UVA or UVB range?
    d) Give one use of ultraviolet radiation.
    e) Give one danger of too much ultraviolet radiation.

41. UVA (315 - 400 nm) can cause premature wrinkling of the skin, while UVB (280 - 315 nm) gives a long lasting tan but can cause sunburn. A sun cream absorbs radiation in the range 9.2×10^{14} Hz to 8.6×10^{14} Hz.
    a) What range of wavelengths is this?
    b) Does this sun cream absorb UVA or UVB radiation?

42. Ultraviolet and infrared travel to the Earth from the Sun at the speed of light. The Sun is 1.5×10^8 km from the Earth.
    a) What is the speed of light?
    b) How long does it take the ultraviolet rays to reach the Earth from the Sun?
    c) How long does it take the infrared rays to reach the Earth from the Sun?

43. The human body emits infrared radiation with wavelengths from 3 μm to 6 μm.
    a) Calculate the range of frequencies emitted.
    b) How is this information used in a thermogram?

44. X-rays travel at the speed of light. They have a range of frequencies from 5×10^{14} Hz to 5×10^{16} Hz.
    a) Calculate the range of wavelengths which correspond to X-rays.
    b) Give a medical use of X-rays.

45. In computer aided tomography, 3-D pictures are built up by taking X-ray pictures of slices through the body. The slice can be 1, 2, 5 or 10 mm thick. A picture of a kidney, which needs to be 10 cm deep, has to be produced. Each slice builds up the image from 1500 detectors and takes 0.5 s. The information from each detector needs 1200 calculations to process the information.
    a) Calculate how many slices are required for the picture if the slices are:
       i) 2 mm thick,   ii) 10 mm thick.
    b) Calculate how long the scan takes for the picture if the slices are:
       i) 2 mm thick,   ii) 10 mm thick.
    c) Find how many calculations are required for the picture if the slices are:
       i) 2 mm thick,   ii) 10 mm thick.
    d) Why is a computer required?

NUCLEAR MEDICINE

46. a) Name the three types of radioactivity.
    b) Which type causes most ionisation?
    c) Describe an experiment which distinguishes between the three types.

47. The following counts per minute were measured in a room when no source was present.

    18, 21, 17, 18, 19, 23, 18, 21, 15, 20

    a) Calculate the average count rate.
    b) Explain why there is a background count rate.
    c) Why is it not constant?

48. The following counts per minute were measured in a room when no source was present.

    29, 31, 27, 35, 22, 28, 31, 28, 30, 29

    a) Calculate the average count rate.
    b) Suggest why this background count rate is much larger than the one in Q. 47.

49. A student obtained the following results when he placed different absorbers between radioactive sources and a Geiger - Muller tube.

Absorbing Material	Count Rate in c.p.m.		
Air only	no source present - 20		
	Source A	Source B	Source C
Air only	678	445	1890
Paper	690	19	1345
Aluminium	682	21	28
Lead	122	18	19

   a) Which source emits only alpha radiation?
   b) What type of radiation is emitted by source C?
   c) Why does the count rate with source A present not come down to the background count rate, even when lead is the absorber?

50. What is the activity of a source in which there are 45 000 atoms decaying in 1 min?

51. What is the activity of a source if there are 17 million atoms decaying in 5 min?

52. If the activity of a source is 25 kBq, how many atoms decay in 30 s?

53. The activity of a source is 3 MBq, how many atoms decay in 5 min?

Standard Grade Physics

HALF LIFE

54. What is meant by the half life of a radioactive substance?

55. The activity of a source drops from 1000 kBq to 125 kBq in 9 days.
    Calculate the half life of the source.

56. The activity of a source drops from 4800 kBq to 150 kBq in 10 days.
    Calculate the half life of the source.

57. The activity of a source drops from 720 MBq to 45 MBq in 20 years.
    Calculate the half life of the source.

58. The activity of a source drops from 4096 kBq to 1 kBq in 2 days.
    Calculate the half life of the source.

59. The activity of a source drops from 448 kBq to 3.5 kBq in 17.5 years.
    Calculate the half life of the source.

60. A source has an activity of 1800 kBq and a half life of 2 days.
    What is its activity 10 days later?

61. A source has an activity of 576 MBq and a half life of 30 years.
    What is its activity 180 years later?

62. A source has an activity of 2400 kBq and a half life of 8 s.
    What is its activity 32 s later?

63. A source has an activity of 3200 kBq and a half life of 5.3 days.
    What is its activity 37.1 days later?

64. A source has an activity of 800 kBq after being stored for 4 days.
    If the half life is 1 day, what was its initial activity?

65. A source has an activity of 1800 kBq after being stored for 72 s.
    If the half life is 24 s, what was its initial activity?

66. A source has an activity of 40 kBq after being stored for 10 years.
    If the half life is 2 years, what was its initial activity?

67. A source has an activity of 30 kBq after being stored for 2 days.
    If the half life is 8 h, what was its initial activity?

68. A source has an activity of 40 MBq and a half life of 15 s.
    How long will it take for its activity to drop to 625 kBq?

69. *A source has an activity of 25 MBq and a half life of 8 days.
    Approximately how long will it take for its activity to drop to below 1MBq?*

70. *A source has an activity of 320 MBq and a half life of 1000 years.
    Approximately how long will it take for its activity to drop to 500 kBq?*

71. A background count rate of 20 counts per minute is measured in the absence of a source. When the source is present the count is 140 counts per minute initially, dropping to 35 counts per minute after 15 days. What is the half life of the source?

72. If the background count is 28 counts per minute and the count with a source drops from 932 to 141 counts per minute in 24 h, what is the half life of the source?

73. If the background count rate is 24 counts per minute and the count rate with a source present drops from 4120 to 25 counts per minute in 2 days, what is the half life of the source?

74. In an experiment with a radioactive source, the count rate corrected for background radiation was measured and the following results obtained.

Time in minutes	Corrected Count Rate in c.p.m.
0	100
1	58
2	32
3	18
4	10
5	5.6

a) Plot a graph to show these results.
b) Estimate the half life of the source from these results.

75. In an experiment with a source, carried out in an area where there is a high background radiation, the following results were obtained.

Time in seconds	Count Rate in c.p.m.
0	88
30	72
60	60
90	52
120	44
150	39
180	36
210	34
240	32
270	29
300	30

a) Plot a graph to show these results.
b) Estimate the background count rate.
c) Estimate the half life of the source from these results.

Standard Grade Physics

ELECTRONICS

OUTPUT DEVICES

1. Draw a trace you could expect on an oscilloscope screen for:
   a) an analogue signal,
   b) a digital signal.

2. Devices can be analogue or digital. Classify the following input devices: microphone, switch, LDR, solar cell, capacitor, thermocouple, thermistor.

3. Devices can be analogue or digital. Classify the following output devices: motor, relay, solenoid, buzzer, loudspeaker, LED, 7-segment display.

4. State which output device you would use in the following situations:
   a) to broadcast the results of a race to the crowd at the track
   b) to show that a piece of equipment is on
   c) to display the time
   d) in the central locking of a car

5. State which output device you would use in the following situations:
   a) to record your voice
   b) to set a motor running when it gets cold
   c) to set a time delay on pedestrian lights
   d) to tell when it gets dark

6. In a seven segment display, the segments are as shown.
   a) State which segments are lit up to show the following numbers:
      i) 4
      ii) 7
      iii) 1
      iv) 2
   b) What number is shown when segments a, b, c, d, g are lit?

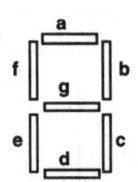

PROTECTIVE RESISTORS

7. An LED takes 10 mA and 1.5 V to work correctly.
   What value of series resistor is required if a 6 V battery is used?

8. An LED takes 15 mA and 2 V to work correctly.
   What value of series resistor is required if a 12 V battery is used?

9. a) An LED takes 10 mA and 2 V to work correctly.
      What value of series resistor is required if a 20 V supply is used?
   b) Draw a circuit diagram showing how the resistor, LED and supply are connected.

10. A 6 V, 12 W light bulb has to be run, at its normal rating, from a 12 V supply as shown.

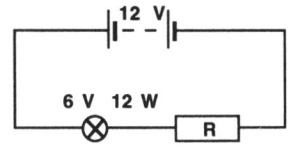

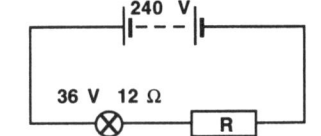

   a) Calculate the current through the bulb.
   b) Calculate the voltage across the resistor.
   c) Calculate the value of the resistor.

11. A 20 V supply is used with an 8 V, 24 W motor and therefore needs a protective resistor.
   a) Calculate the current through the motor.
   b) Calculate the voltage across the resistor.
   c) Calculate the resistance required.

12. A 120 V, 60 W motor is used with a 240V supply.
   Calculate the value of the resistor which should be used to run it at its normal rating.

13. A 240 V supply is used to run a 36 V, 18 Ω bulb as shown.
   a) Calculate the current through the bulb.
   b) Calculate the voltage across the resistor.
   c) Calculate the value of the resistor.

14. A 1.5 V cell is used with a 300 mV, 75 Ω component.
   What protective resistor is required?

15. A 12 V supply is used with a 3 V, 6 W bulb. In order to protect it a 3 Ω resistor has been placed in series.
   What additional series resistance would be needed to protect the bulb properly?

16. A 500 V supply gives a current of 5 A for a large motor. The motor has a resistance of 95 Ω.
   a) Explain why a protective resistor is required.
   b) Calculate the value.

17. An LED requires 10^{-2} A and 3.2 V to work correctly.
   a) What protective resistor is required with a 9 V supply?
   b) Calculate the resistance of the LED.
   c) Calculate the power rating of the LED.

Standard Grade Physics

VOLTAGE DIVIDERS

$$V_{R_1} = \frac{R_1}{R_{total}} \times V_{supply}$$

18. Find the voltages V_1 and V_2 in the following circuits:

a) 6 V, 6 Ω (V_2), 6 Ω (V_1)

b) 12 V, 4 Ω (V_2), 2 Ω (V_1)

c) 8 V, 9 Ω (V_2), 3 Ω (V_1)

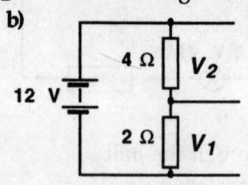

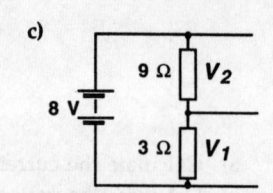

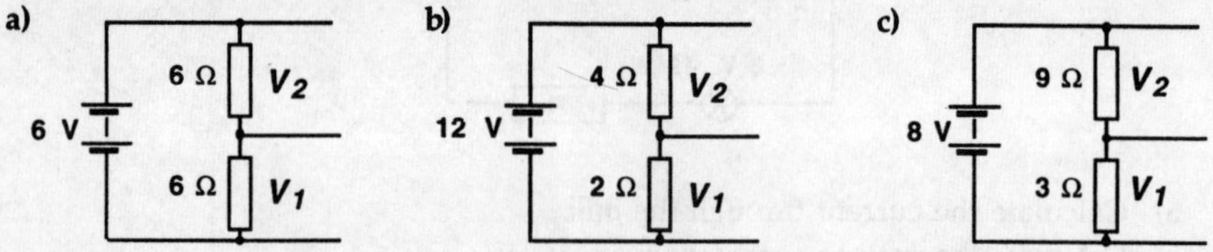

19. Find the voltages V_1 and V_2 in the following circuits:

a) 2.5 V, 3.7 Ω (V_2), 8.3 Ω (V_1)

b) 72 V, 2 kΩ (V_2), 800 Ω (V_1)

c) 24 V, 80 kΩ (V_2), 100 kΩ (V_1)

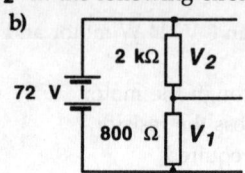

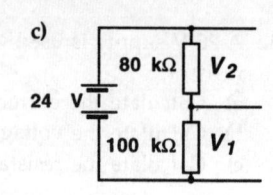

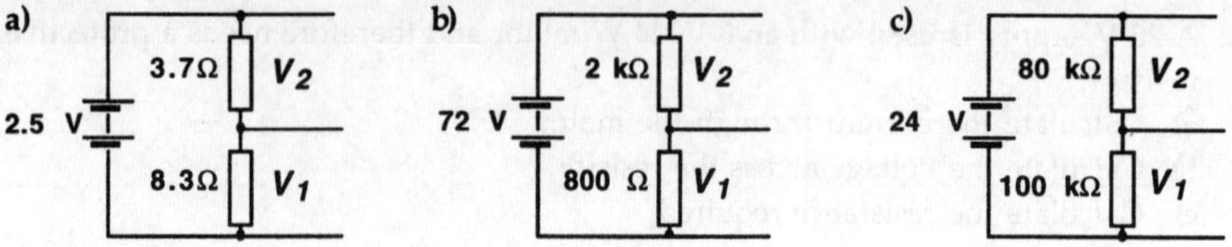

20. Find the resistance R_1 and the voltage V_1 in the following circuits:

a) 12 V, 8 Ω (2 V), R_1 (V_1)

b) 24 V, 150 Ω (18 V), R_1 (V_1)

c) 9 V, 10 Ω (4.8 V), R_1 (V_1)

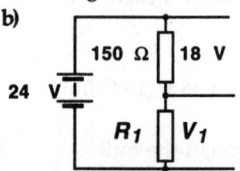

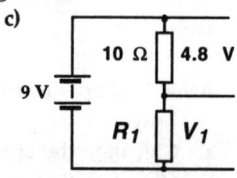

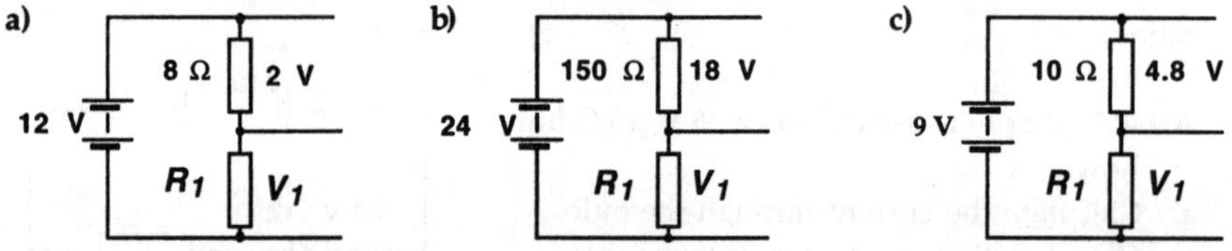

21. Find the resistance R_2 and the voltage V_1 in the following circuits:

a) 1 kV, R_2 (450 V), 3.3 kΩ (V_1)

b) 80 V, R_2 (68 V), 48 Ω (V_1)

c) 56 V, R_2 (24 V), 2 kΩ (V_1)

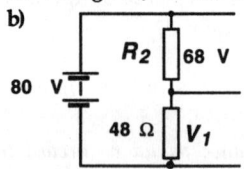

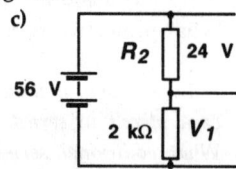

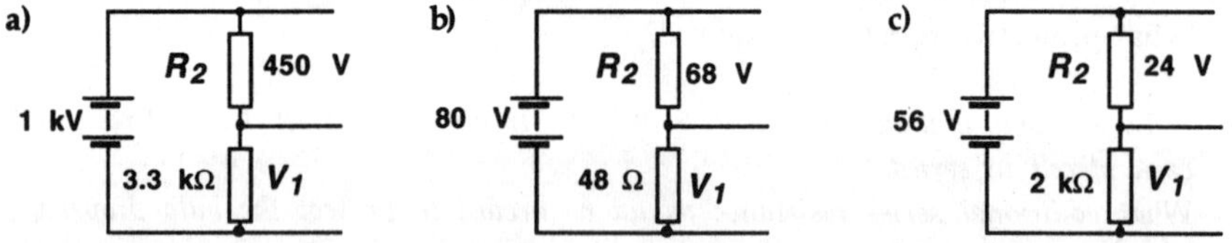

22. Find the voltages V_1, V_2 and V_3 in the following circuits:

a) 24 V, 4 Ω (V_3), 4 Ω (V_2), 4 Ω (V_1)

b) 1 kV, 6 kΩ (V_3), 4 kΩ (V_2), 2 kΩ (V_1)

c) 75 V, 1 MΩ (V_3), 3 MΩ (V_2), 2 MΩ (V_1)

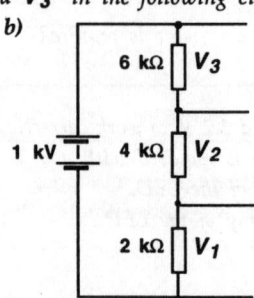

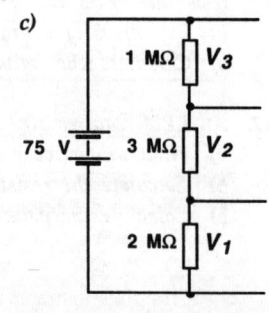

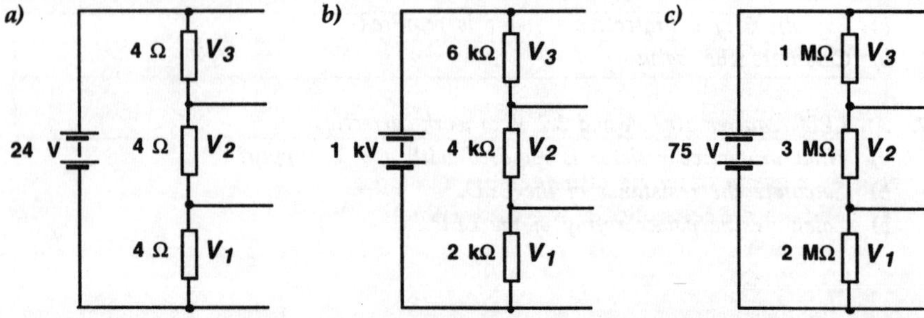

23. Find the voltages V_1, V_2 and V_3 in the following circuits:

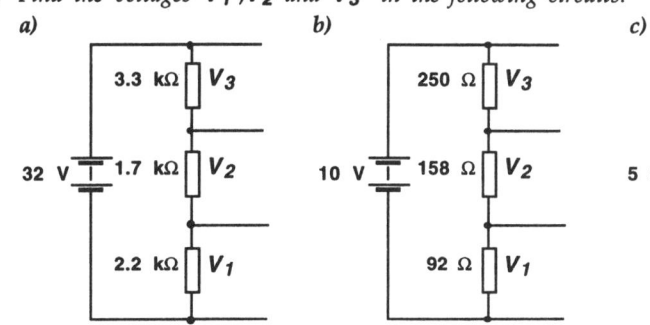

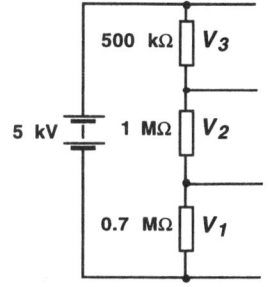

a) 32 V battery with 3.3 kΩ (V_3), 1.7 kΩ (V_2), 2.2 kΩ (V_1) in series.

b) 10 V battery with 250 Ω (V_3), 158 Ω (V_2), 92 Ω (V_1) in series.

c) 5 kV battery with 500 kΩ (V_3), 1 MΩ (V_2), 0.7 MΩ (V_1) in series.

24. Find the voltages V_1, V_2 and V_3 in the following circuits:

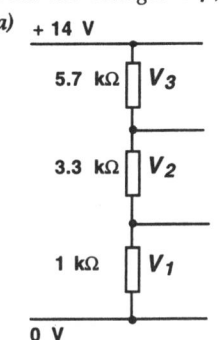

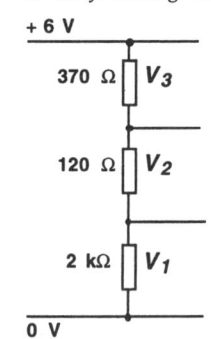

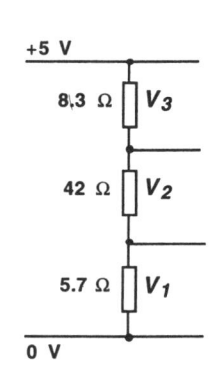

a) +14 V supply with 5.7 kΩ (V_3), 3.3 kΩ (V_2), 1 kΩ (V_1) to 0 V.

b) +6 V supply with 370 Ω (V_3), 120 Ω (V_2), 2 kΩ (V_1) to 0 V.

c) +5 V supply with 8.3 Ω (V_3), 42 Ω (V_2), 5.7 Ω (V_1) to 0 V.

THERMISTORS AND LDRS

25. What happens to the resistance of a thermistor as the temperature increases?

26. What happens to the resistance of the LDR as the light intensity decreases?

27. A thermistor was used as the input of an electronic thermometer. In order to calibrate the thermometer, resistance was measured at various known temperatures and the following results were obtained.

Temperature in °C	0	30	60	90	120	150	180
Resistance in Ω	1240	675	480	360	255	195	150

a) Plot a graph of temperature against resistance.
b) Estimate the resistance of the thermistor at
   i) 100 °C,
   ii) 75 °C.
c) If the thermistor is connected directly across a 12 V battery, what would the current be when the temperature is 37 °C?

Standard Grade Physics 47

28. An LDR was calibrated against known light intensities and the following results obtained.

Light Intensity in units	100	300	500	700	900
Resistance in Ω	4000	1300	690	460	370

a) Plot a graph of temperature against light intensity.
b) Estimate the light intensity of the LDR when the resistance is:
  i) 1500 Ω,
  ii) 500 Ω.
c) If the LDR is connected directly across a 5 V battery, state what the current would be when the light intensity is:
  i) 400 units,
  ii) 600 units.

29. A thermistor was connected in a circuit as shown. The resistance of the themistor at various temperatures is shown in the table.

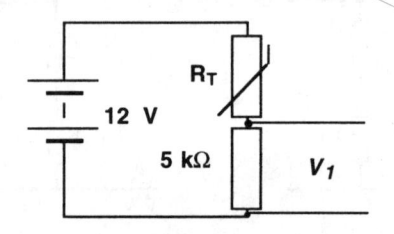

Temperature	Resistance of R_T
50 °C	10 kΩ
100 °C	3 kΩ
200 °C	2.2 kΩ

a) Calculate the current when the temperature is 50 °C.
b) Calculate V_1 when the temperature is 200 °C.
c) Calculate the current when the temperature is 100 °C.
d) Estimate the current when the temperature is 75 °C.

30. An LDR was connected in a circuit as shown. The resistance of the LDR at various light levels is shown in the table.

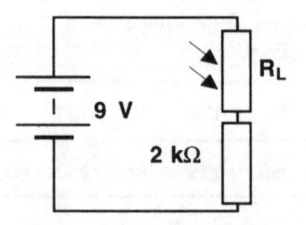

Light Level	Resistance of R_L
2.5 units	1800 Ω
5 units	800 Ω
10 units	520 Ω
20 units	400 Ω

a) Calculate the current when the light level is 2.5 units.
b) Calculate the current when the light level is 5 units.
c) Calculate the current when the light level is 10 units.
d) Calculate the current when the light level is 20 units.
e) Estimate the current when the light level is 30 units.

CAPACITORS

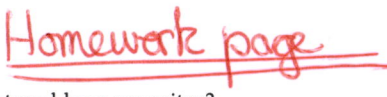

Homework page

31. What **two** quantities are stored by a capacitor?

32. A capacitor and resistor are connected in series as shown. Various values for both **R** and **C** are used as shown in the table in part **b)**. In each case the time taken to reach 12 V across the capacitor was measured.

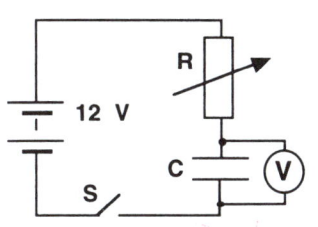

a) To increase the time necessary to fully charge the capacitor to 12 V, state whether
   i) the resistance should be increased or decreased,
   ii) the capacitance should be increased or decreased.

b) *The time taken for it to be fully charged is given by the 'time constant' which is found by multiplying the resistance by the capacitance. Complete the following table:*

	Resistance	Capacitance	Time
i)	100 kΩ	1 µF	-----
ii)	-----	10 µF	1 s
iii)	100 kΩ	100 µF	-----
iv)	1000 kΩ	10 µF	-----
v)	10 MΩ	10 µF	-----
vi)	1 kΩ	-----	1 s

33. The voltage across a capacitor was measured every second. The readings are shown.

Voltage in V	0	4	7.2	10	12.1	14	15	15.8	16	16	16
Time in s	0	1	2	3	4	5	6	7	8	9	10	11

a) Plot a graph of voltage against time.
b) What is the voltage of the battery?
c) What changes could you make to the circuit to increase the time taken for the voltage across the capacitor to reach 16 V?

34. Suggest a possible use for a capacitor and resistor combination as an input device.

35. a) Sketch a graph to show how the voltage across the capacitor varies with time, from the instant that the switch is closed.
   b) What will be the final voltage across the capacitor?

Standard Grade Physics

SWITCHING CIRCUITS

Homework pg

36.

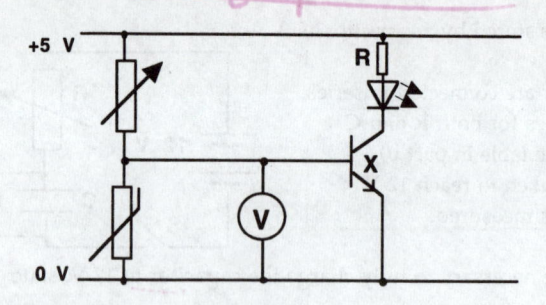

a) Name the component labelled **X**.
b) What happens to the voltage across the thermistor as the temperature decreases?
c) Approximately, what voltage is required for the LED to light?
d) What is the function of the resistor **R**?
e) Why is a variable resistor used?
f) Suggest a use for this circuit.

37.

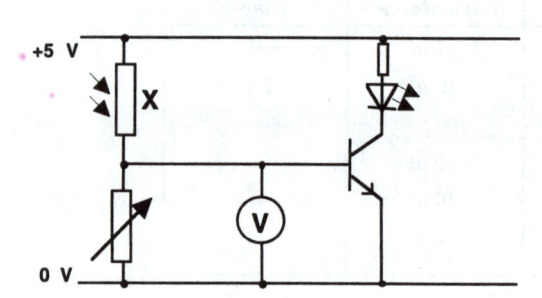

a) Name the component labelled **X**.
b) What happens to the voltage across the LDR as the light intensity increases?
c) What happens to the voltage across the variable resistor as the light intensity increases?
d) When will the LED light, as it gets dark or as it gets light?
e) What change could be made to the circuit to allow the other possibility mentioned in part **d)**?
f) Suggest a use for this circuit.

38. Draw a circuit which would switch on a buzzer and sound an alarm if a greenhouse was over heating.

39. Draw a circuit which would use a motor to open curtains as soon as it was fully light.

40.

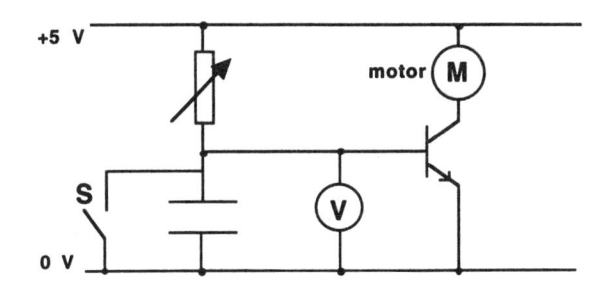

a) What is the function of the switch S?
b) What happens to the voltage across the capacitor when the switch is first opened?
c) When will the motor come on?
d) Why is a variable resistor included?
e) Suggest a use for this circuit.

41. A courtesy light in a car can be connected as shown.

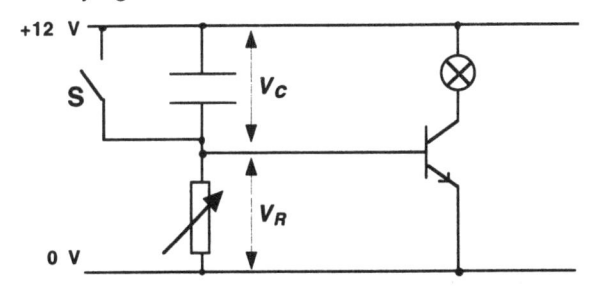

When the car door is shut, switch S is open.

a) i) Is the capacitor charged or discharged?
   ii) What is the voltage V_R?
   iii) What is the voltage V_C?
   iv) Is the courtesy light on or off?

b) The car door opens and the switch closes.
   i) What happens to the capacitor?
   ii) What is the final voltage V_R?
   iii) What is the final voltage V_C?
   iv) Is the courtesy light on or off?

Standard Grade Physics

LOGIC GATES

42. a) Draw the symbol for the NOT gate.
    b) Give the truth table for the NOT gate.

43. a) Draw the symbol for the AND gate.
    b) Give the truth table for the AND gate.

44. a) Draw the symbol for the OR gate.
    b) Give the truth table for the OR gate.

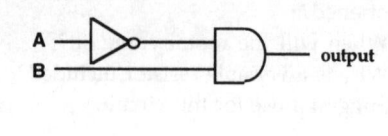

45. Complete the truth table for the combination of gates shown:

A	B	output
0	0	
0	1	
1	0	
1	1	

46. Complete the truth table for the combination of gates shown:

A	B	output
0	0	
0	1	
1	0	
1	1	

47. Complete the truth table for the combination of gates shown:

A	B	C	D	E	output
0	0	0			
0	0	1			
0	1	0			
0	1	1			
1	0	0			
1	0	1			
1	1	0			
1	1	1			

48.

Complete the truth table for the combination of gates shown:

A	B	C	D	E	output
0	0	0	0	1	0
0	0	1	0	1	1
0	1	0	1	0	0
0	1	1	1	0	0
1	0	0	1	0	0
1	0	1	1	0	0
1	1	0	1	0	0
1	1	1	1	0	0

49.

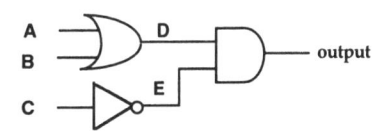

Complete the truth table for the combination of gates shown:

A	B	C	D	E	output
0	0	0	0	1	0
0	0	1	0	0	0
0	1	0	1	1	1
0	1	1	1	0	0
1	0	0	1	1	1
1	0	1	1	0	0
1	1	0	1	1	1
1	1	1	1	0	0

50.

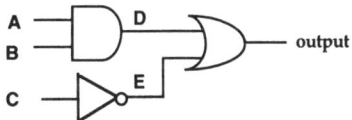

Complete the truth table for the combination of gates shown:

A	B	C	D	E	output
0	0	0	0	1	1
0	0	1	0	0	0
0	1	0	0	1	1
0	1	1	0	0	0
1	0	0	0	1	1
1	0	1	0	0	0
1	1	0	1	1	1
1	1	1	1	0	1

Standard Grade Physics

51. *Draw up the truth table for the combination of gates shown:*

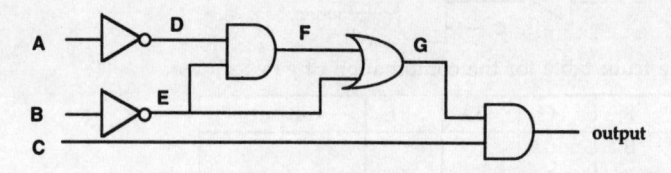

52. *Draw up the truth table for the combination of gates shown:*

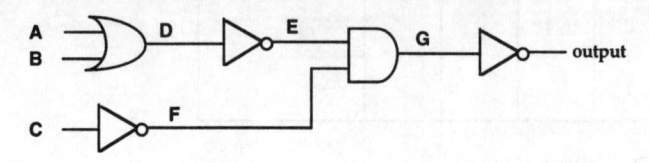

53. A light sensor gives a logic '1' when it is dark and a temperature sensor gives a logic '1' when it is hot. Design a logic circuit which would turn on a motor to open greenhouse windows when it is daylight **and** gets too hot.

54. Design a logic circuit which will allow a display cabinet to be opened, only if:
the main switch is on,
the alarm button is **not** pressed,
the switch for the cabinet is pressed.

55. Design a logic circuit which allows a washing machine motor to switch on, only if:
the water reaches a certain level (pressure sensor gives logic '1'),
the water is up to temperature (temperature sensor gives logic '0'),
the door is shut (switch gives logic '1').

56. A security system has to activate an alarm, only if:
it is dark (light sensor give logic '1' when it is light),
the main control switch has been set (switch gives logic '1' when on),
an intruder is sensed by a movement sensor (movement sensor gives logic '1' when there is movement).
Design the logic system which would be required.

57. A motor has a cut off system which protects the motor from damage. The cut off only works if the motor is running **and** it has overheated for more than 10 s. Design a logic circuit to do this and suggest suitable input devices.

58. A hi-fi system has to operate a lighting display, so that the lights flash every time the sound level reaches a certain volume, **or** it has been more than 10 s since the previous flash.
Design a logic circuit to do this and suggest suitable input and output devices.

CLOCK PULSE GENERATORS

59. The circuit for a clock pulse generator is shown.

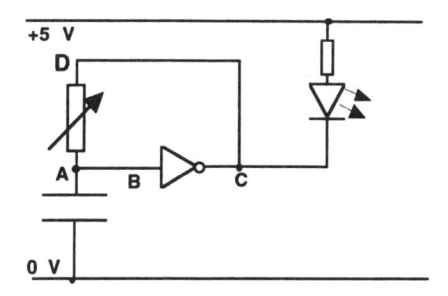

   a) The capacitor is initially uncharged.
      i) What is the voltage at **A**?
      ii) What is the logic level at **B**?
      iii) What is the logic level at **C**?
      iv) What is the voltage at **D**?
   b) i) What happens to the capacitor?
      ii) What is the voltage at **A** now?
      iii) What is the logic level at **B** now?
      iv) What is the logic level at **C** now?
      v) What is the voltage at **D** now?
   c) What happens to the capacitor?
   d) Why does this give pulses?

60. a) Sketch the output from a clock pulse generator with a capacitor of 10 µF and a resistor of 100 kΩ (medium **C** and **R**).
    b) Sketch the output which would be produced with a capacitor of 100 µF and a resistor of 1000 kΩ (large **C** and **R**).
    c) Sketch the output which would be produced with a capacitor of 1 µF and a resistor of 10 kΩ (small **C** and **R**).

61. A counter circuit can be used in a calculator but the output is in binary and has to be converted into decimal. Give the decimal equivalents of:
    a) 1001,
    b) 1101,
    c) 0110,
    d) 100101,
    e) 10101001.

62. Give the binary equivalents of:
    a) 7,
    b) 11,
    c) 31,
    d) 275,
    e) 1436.

Standard Grade Physics

ANALOGUE PROCESSES

63. State the effect that an amplifier has on:
    a) the frequency of the signal,
    b) the amplitude of the signal.

64. Copy the following signal onto graph paper and then on the same graph paper show the signal which would be produced if it was amplified 4 times:

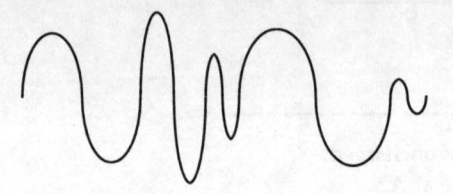

65. Using the same initial signal as Q. 64 show the output which would be produced if it was amplified by a factor of 0.5.

VOLTAGE GAIN

$$\text{voltage gain} = \frac{\text{output voltage}}{\text{input voltage}}$$

66. Complete the following table:

	INPUT VOLTAGE	OUTPUT VOLTAGE	VOLTAGE GAIN
a)	100 V	3 kV	-------
b)	-------	50 V	6×10^3
c)	58 mV	-------	9.2×10^2
d)	-------	9.6 V	3×10^{-2}
e)	116.8 µV	8.76 V	-------
f)	5.6 mV	-------	10^4

67. What input voltage gives an output voltage of 24 V from an amplifier with a voltage gain of 300?

68. If the input voltage to an amplifier is 360 µV and the output voltage is 48 V, calculate the voltage gain of the amplifier.

69. The voltage gain of an amplfier is 1900 and the input voltage to it is 23 mV. Calculate the output voltage from the amplifier.

70. An input voltage of 700 µV produces an output current of 1.5 A.
    If the output resistance is 13 Ω, what is the voltage gain?

POWER, VOLTAGE AND RESISTANCE $P = \dfrac{V^2}{R}$

71. Complete the following table (also see page 20):

	POWER	VOLTAGE	RESISTANCE
a)	36 W	-------	16 Ω
b)	-------	240 V	7×10^3 Ω
c)	90 W	5 V	-------
d)	-------	75 mV	9 Ω
e)	15 kW	-------	8 kΩ
f)	1.5 mW	45 mV	-------

72. An amplifier has an input resistance of 28 kΩ and an input voltage of 9 mV. What is the input power?

73. An amplifier has an input power of 56 μW and has an input resistance of 9 kΩ. What is the input voltage?

74. An amplifer with an input voltage of 17 mV provides an input power of 7 μW. What is the input resistance?

POWER GAIN   power gain = $\dfrac{\text{output power}}{\text{input power}}$

75. Complete the following table:

	INPUT POWER	OUTPUT POWER	POWER GAIN
a)	36 mW	-------	6×10^3
b)	-------	240 W	9.6×10^5
c)	7.2 μW	8 kW	-------
d)	-------	125 W	2.5×10^6
e)	6.3 mW	-------	10^5
f)	8 mW	72 W	-------

76. What is the power gain of an amplifier, if an input power of 3mW produces an output power of 6×10^2 W?

77. If the power gain of an amplifier is 10^4, what input power gives an output power of 37.5 W?

Standard Grade Physics

MIXED PROBLEMS ON AMPLFIERS

78. The input voltage to an amplifier is 9 mV and the output voltage is 27 V. The input resistance is 24 kΩ and the output resistance is 96 Ω.
    a) Calculate the voltage gain of the amplifier.
    b) Calculate the input power to the amplifier.
    c) Calculate the ouput power from the amplifier.
    d) Calculate the power gain of the amplifier.
    e) Where does the energy for this extra power come from?

79. The input voltage to an amplifier is 10^{-3} V and the output voltage is 3.6 V. The input resistance is 10^4 Ω and the output resistance is 9 Ω.
    a) Calculate the voltage gain of the amplifier.
    b) Calculate the input power to the amplifier.
    c) Calculate the ouput power from the amplifier.
    d) Calculate the power gain of the amplifier.

80. An amplifier has an input resistance of 18 kΩ and receives an input voltage of 9 mV. If the power output is 84 W, calculate the power gain of the amplifier.

81. An amplifier delivers 64 W to a loudspeaker of resistance 8 Ω.
    Calculate the potential difference (voltage) across the loudspeaker.

82. An amplifier delivers 96 W to a loudspeaker of resistance 16 Ω.
    If the input voltage to the amplifier is 24 mV, calculate the voltage gain.

83. An amplifier delivers 11 W to a loudspeaker of resistance 396 Ω.
    If the input voltage to the amplifier is 33 mV, calculate the voltage gain.

84. An amplifier has an input signal of 400 μV, an input resistance of 18 kΩ and an output power of 68 W. Calculate the power gain.

85. An amplifier has an input signal of 9.2 mV, an input resistance of 65 kΩ and an output power of 56 W. Calculate the power gain.

86. An amplifier has a power gain of 3×10^7 and produces an output power of 27 W. If the input voltage is 3.6 mV, what is the input resistance?

87. An amplifier has a power gain of 6×10^6. It produces an output power of 72 W. If the input voltage is 4.8 mV, what is the input resistance?

88. An amplifier has a voltage gain of 5×10^4 and produces an output power of 32 W. If the input voltage is 90 μV, what is the output resistance?

TRANSPORT

AVERAGE AND INSTANTANEOUS SPEED

1. A car travels 500 m in 30 s. Calculate its average speed.

2. A man walks 1 km in 10 min. Calculate his average speed.

3. A car is travelling at 90 km h^{-1} when the driver looks at the speedometer. However, it takes 3 h to travel 200 km.
    a) What is the average speed in kilometres per hour?
    b) Why is the instantaneous speed different from the average speed?
    c) What is the instantaneous speed in metres per second?

4. A train is travelling from Aberdeen to Inverness. Part of the train timetable is shown below.

Aberdeen	dep.	0628	
Inverurie	arr.	0650	19 km
	dep.	0705	
Elgin	arr.	0804	65 km
	dep.	0819	
Inverness	arr.	0857	81 km

    a) Calculate the average speed in kilometres per hour from Aberdeen to Inverurie.
    b) Calculate the average speed in kilometres per hour from Inverurie to Elgin.
    c) Calculate the average speed in kilometres per hour from Elgin to Inverness.
    d) Calculate the average speed in kilometres per hour from Aberdeen to Inverness.
    e) Calculate the average speed in metres per second from Aberdeen to Inverness.

5. A train is travelling from Glasgow to Edinburgh. Part of the train timetable is shown below.

Glasgow	dep.	1800	
Falkirk	arr.	1820	28 km
	dep.	1830	
Linlithgow	arr.	1838	12 km
	dep.	1840	
Edinburgh	arr.	1905	34 km

    a) Calculate the average speed in kilometres per hour from Glasgow to Falkirk.
    b) Calculate the average speed in kilometres per hour from Falkirk to Linlithgow.
    c) Calculate the average speed in kilometres per hour from Linlithgow to Edinburgh.
    d) Calculate the average speed in kilometres per hour from Glasgow to Edinburgh.
    e) Calculate the average speed in metres per second from Glasgow to Edinburgh.

Standard Grade Physics

6. **a)** A train is travelling from Dingwall to Kyle of Lochalsh. Part of the train timetable is shown below:

Dingwall	dep.	1111	
Achnasheen	arr.	1200	42 km
	dep.	1205	
Stromeferry	arr.	1250	42 km
	dep.	1252	
Kyle of Lochalsh	arr.	1315	18 km

   i) Calculate the average speed in kilometres per hour from Dingwall to Achnasheen.
   ii) Calculate the average speed in kilometres per hour from Achnasheen to Stromeferry.
   iii) Calculate the average speed in kilometres per hour from Stromeferry to Kyle of Lochalsh.

   b) A second train goes from Dingwall to Kyle of Lochalsh in 1 h 30 min.
   i) Suggest a reason why it might be faster.
   ii) Calculate the average speed in metres per second of the second train from Dingwall to Kyle of Lochalsh.

7. A plane leaves London at 7.25 G.M.T. and arrives in New York at 12.10 G.M.T.
   a) How long did the plane take for the journey?
   b) If it is 5100 km from London to New York, calculate the average speed
   i) in kilometres per hour,
   ii) in metres per second.
   c) The return journey takes 4 h 15 min.
   What is the average speed in kilometres per hour for this journey?
   d) Suggest why the two average speeds might be different.

8. A ship takes 5 days and 19 h to travel from San Francisco to Honolulu. If the distance is 3885 km, calculate the average speed:
   a) in kilometres per hour,
   b) in metres per second.

9. A ship travels at an average speed of 28 km h^{-1} and takes 3 days and 19 h to travel from Glasgow to Gibraltar. How far does it travel?

10. A ship travels at an average speed of 42 km h^{-1} and takes 8 days and 5 h to travel from New Orleans to London. How far does it travel?

ACCELERATION $a = \frac{v-u}{t}$

11. Complete the following table:

	INITIAL VELOCITY	FINAL VELOCITY	TIME	ACCELERATION
a)	20 m s^{-1}	50 m s^{-1}	10 s	-------
b)	100 m s^{-1}	10 m s^{-1}	3 s	-------
c)	0 m s^{-1}	25 m s^{-1}	----	5 m s^{-2}
d)	48 m s^{-1}	12 m s^{-1}	----	-3 m s^{-2}
e)	-------	28 m s^{-1}	3 s	7 m s^{-2}
f)	8 m s^{-1}	-------	15 s	6 m s^{-2}
g)	-------	75 m s^{-1}	18 s	3.5 m s^{-2}
h)	9.3 m s^{-1}	-------	12.5 s	6.2 m s^{-2}

12. A trolley takes 7.5 s to reach 6 m s^{-1} from rest. Calculate the acceleration.

13. A bus travelling at 12 m s^{-1} slows to rest in 9 s. Calculate the acceleration.

14. If a ball is travelling at 43 m s^{-1} after accelerating at 10 m s^{-2} for 3 s, what was its initial speed?

15. A boy on a skateboard is travelling at 5 m s^{-1} when he starts down a steep hill and accelerates at 2.3 m s^{-2} for 7 s. What is his final speed?

16. A car decelerates at 1.5 m s^{-2} for 14 s from an initial speed of 27 m s^{-1}. What is the final speed?

17. What is the final speed of a rocket which accelerates at 200 m s^{-1} from rest for 3.5 s?

18. A supertanker travelling at 13 m s^{-1} decelerates at 0.02 m s^{-2}. How long does it take to come to a complete stop?

19. A van travelling at 50 km h^{-1} decelerates at 2.5 m s^{-2} to a stop.
    a) What is the initial speed of the van in metres per second?
    b) How long does it take to come to a stop?

20. What is the initial speed of a car which has accelerated at 3.25 m s^{-2} for 9 s to reach a final speed of 40 m s^{-1}?

SPEED TIME GRAPHS

21. For each of the following graphs:

    a) [Graph: speed rises from 0 to 12 m s⁻¹ at t=5s, constant to t=10s]

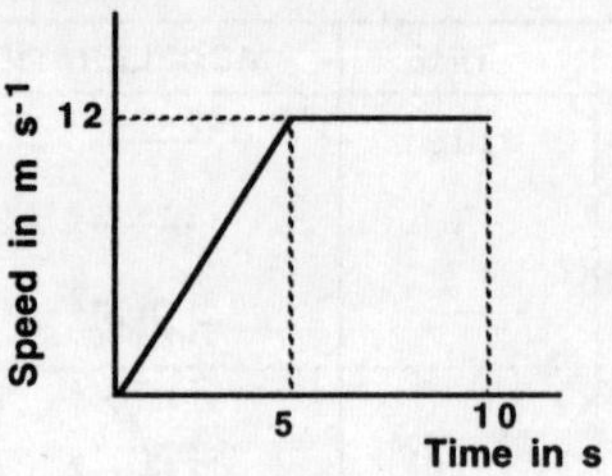

    b) [Graph: speed rises from 0 to 27 m s⁻¹ at t=3s, constant to t=9s]

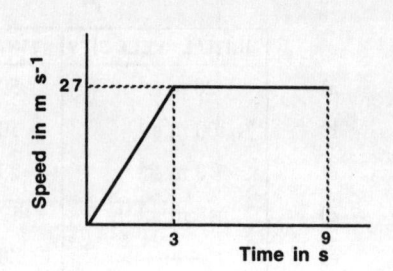

    i) calculate the initial acceleration,
    ii) calculate the total distance travelled,
    iii) calculate the average speed.

22. For each of the following graphs:

    a) [Graph: speed rises from 0 to 25 m s⁻¹ at t=5s, constant to t=10s, falls to 0 at t=14s]

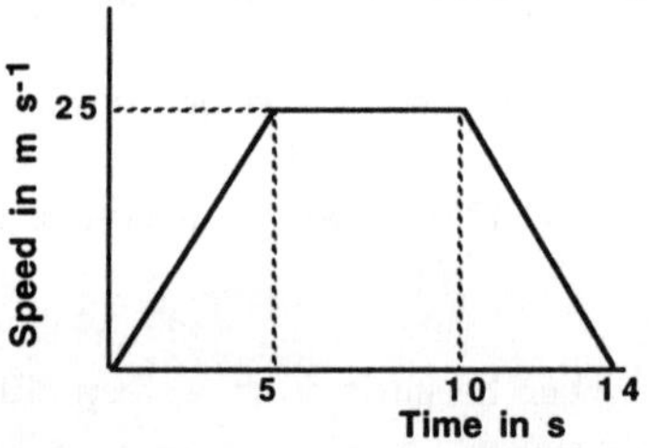

    b) [Graph: speed rises from 0 to 15 m s⁻¹ at t=3s, constant to t=9s, falls to 0 at t=11s]

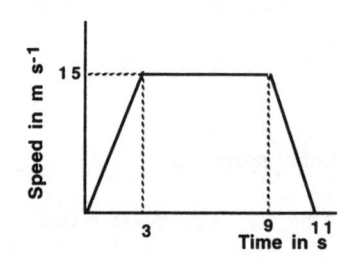

    i) calculate the initial acceleration,
    ii) calculate the final deceleration,
    iii) calculate the total distance travelled,
    iv) calculate the average speed.

23. For each of the following graphs:

    a) [Graph: speed rises from 8 to 12 m s⁻¹ between t=0 and t=2s, constant to t=4s, rises to 30 m s⁻¹ at t=6s, constant to t=9s, falls to 0 at t=12s]

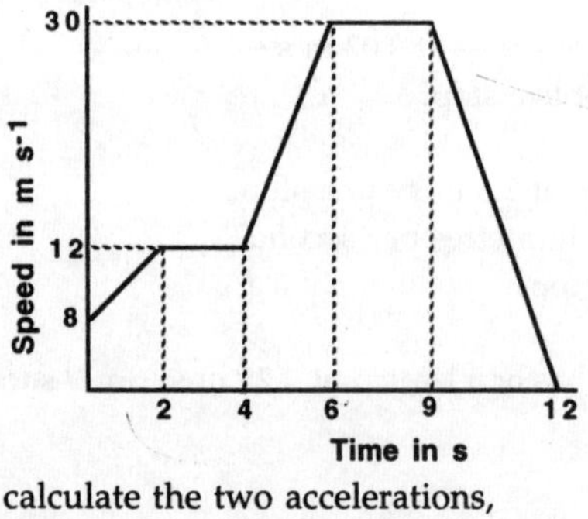

    b) [Graph: speed rises from 2 to 7 m s⁻¹ between t=0 and t=2s, constant to t=5s, rises to 18 m s⁻¹ at t=8s, falls to 12 m s⁻¹ at t=12s, constant to t=16s]

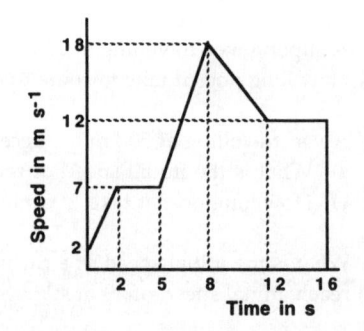

    i) calculate the two accelerations,
    ii) calculate the final deceleration,
    iii) calculate the total distance travelled,
    iv) calculate the average speed.

62   Numerical Questions for

24. Consider the following graph of the motion of a model car.

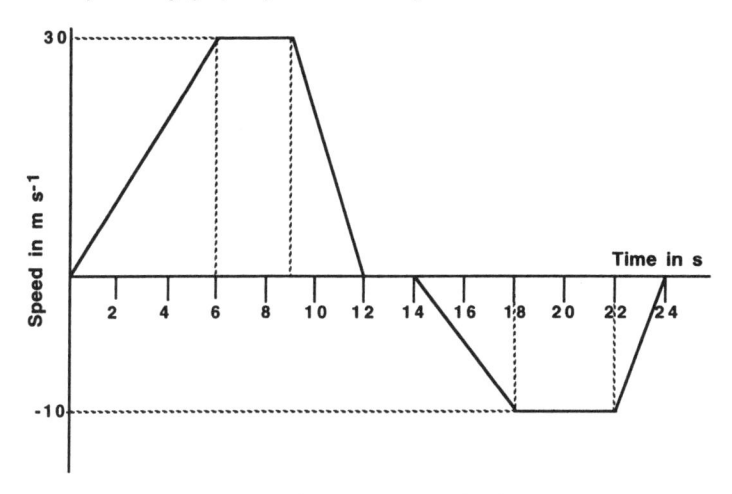

a) Describe the motion of the car between 12 s and 14 s?
b) What can you say about the direction of the motion between 0 and 12 s compared to that between 14 and 24 s?
c) Calculate the initial acceleration.
d) Calculate the deceleration between 9 s and 12 s.
e) Calculate the total distance travelled.
f) Calculate the average speed.
g) How far does the model car finish from the start?

25. Consider the following graph of the motion of a trolley.

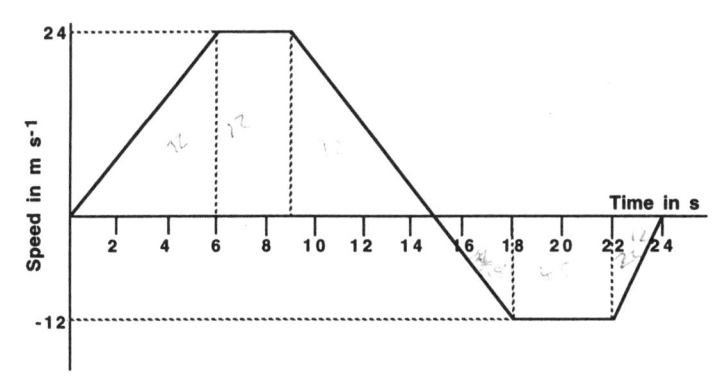

a) Calculate the initial acceleration.
b) Calculate the deceleration between 9 s and 15 s.
c) Calculate the total distance travelled.
d) Calculate the average speed.
e) How far does the trolley finish from the start?

WEIGHT $W = mg$ (Assume g on Earth is 10 N kg^{-1}.)

26. Complete the following table:

	WEIGHT	MASS	GRAVITATIONAL FIELD STRENGTH
a)	100 N	10 kg	-------
b)	-------	4 kg	10 N kg^{-1}
c)	4.8 N	-------	1.6 N kg^{-1}
d)	7.5 N	288 g	-------
e)	-------	750 mg	3.8 N kg^{-1}
f)	65 kN	-------	274 N kg^{-1}

27. Calculate the weight on Earth of the following masses:
    a) 9500 kg,
    b) 10^{-7} kg,
    c) 27 g,
    d) 10^{-3} g.

28. Calculate the mass of objects with weights on Earth of:
    a) 787 N,
    b) 0.375 N,
    c) 1×10^{-4} N,
    d) 689 kN.

29. When g varies, is it the mass or the weight which remains constant?

30. A man has a mass of 70 kg on Earth.
    a) What is the man's weight on Earth?
    b) What would be the mass of the man on Mars, where g = 3.8 N kg^{-1}?
    c) What would be the weight of the man on Mars?

31. A satellite has a mass of 900 kg on Earth.
    a) What is the satellite's weight on Earth?
    b) What would be the mass of the satellite on Jupiter, where g = 26 N kg^{-1}?
    c) What would be the weight of the satellite on Jupiter?

32. A meteorite has a weight of 15 N on Earth.
    a) What is the meteorite's mass on Earth?
    b) What would be the mass of the meteorite on Mars, where g = 3.8 N kg^{-1}?
    c) What would be the weight of the meteorite on Mars?

33. An object has a weight of 0.35 N on Earth.
    a) What is the object's mass on Earth?
    b) What would be the mass of the object on Jupiter, where g = 26 N kg^{-1}?
    c) What would be the weight of the object on Jupiter?

NEWTON'S FIRST LAW   (Assume g on Earth is 10 N kg^{-1}.)

34. A box is hanging on a rope and has a mass of 3.8 kg.
    a) Calculate its weight.
    b) Calculate the tension (force) in the rope.

35. Two men earn their living on the trapeze in a circus. Marcus has a mass of 59 kg. What force does Johann have to exert to support his partner Marcus while he is at rest?

36. A rocket is moving up from Earth at a steady speed of 400 m s^{-1}. It has a mass of 2340 kg. What force must the rocket engine be exerting?

37. A car driver keeps his foot on the accelerator but the car does not accelerate, it just continues at the same speed. Explain this.

38. A rocket is fired from Earth and reaches a speed of 12 000 km s^{-1} as it leaves the Earth's gravitational field. Its engine is then switched off as it heads off towards Saturn.
    a) What will its speed be in 24 h?
    b) Explain your answer to part a).

39. A box slides down a slope at a constant speed as shown. Calculate the value **F**.

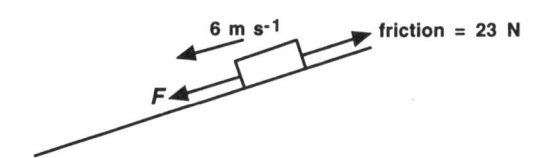

    6 m s^{-1} friction = 23 N
    F

40. What force must be exerted to move a 2.6 kg box vertically upwards at 3 m s^{-1}?

41. a) What force must be exerted to move a 97.5 g ball vertically upwards at 9.5 m s^{-1}?
    b) What assumption is being made?

42. What force is applied to move a mass of 10^7 kg vertically off Earth at a constant speed of 1200 m s^{-1}?

43. A balloon of mass 586 kg moves up at a constant speed of 0.25 m s^{-1}. Calculate the buoyancy force.

44. A force of 11.5 kN is exerted to move an object vertically upwards at a constant speed of 3.5 m s^{-1}. What is the mass of the object?

45. A force of 0.3 N is exerted to move a ball of mass 30 g vertically upwards. If the initial speed is 15 m s^{-1}, calculate the speed 6 s later.

Standard Grade Physics

RESULTANT FORCE (Assume g on Earth is 10 N kg^{-1}.)

46. Calculate the resultant force of the following, giving both size and direction of the resultant:

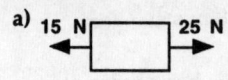

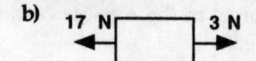

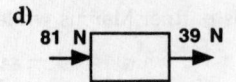

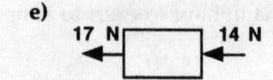

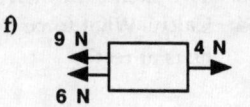

   a) 15 N ← ☐ → 25 N
   b) 17 N ← ☐ → 3 N
   c) 9 N ← ☐ → 12 N
   d) 81 N → ☐ ← 39 N
   e) 17 N ← ☐ ← 14 N
   f) 9 N ← ☐ → 4 N, 6 N ↓

47. Calculate the net force of the following, giving both size and direction of the resultant:

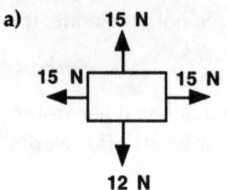

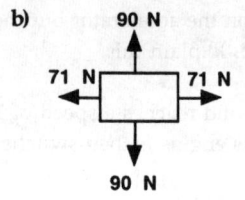

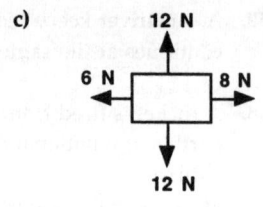

   a) 15 N ↑, 15 N ←, 15 N →, 12 N ↓
   b) 90 N ↑, 71 N ←, 71 N →, 90 N ↓
   c) 12 N ↑, 6 N ←, 8 N →, 12 N ↓

48. The rocket has a mass of 4×10^4 kg.
   a) Calculate the weight of the rocket on the Earth's surface.
   b) Calculate the resultant vertical force on the rocket.

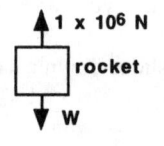

   1×10^6 N ↑ rocket, W ↓

49. The balloon has a total mass of 950 kg.
   a) Calculate the weight of the balloon on the Earth's surface.
   b) Calculate the resultant vertical force on the balloon.

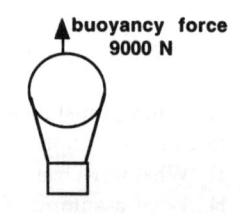

   buoyancy force 9000 N ↑

NEWTON'S SECOND LAW $F = ma$

50. Complete the following table (1 tonne = 1000 kg):

	MASS	ACCELERATION	FORCE
a)	3 kg	4 m s^{-2}	-------
b)	-------	12 m s^{-2}	6 N
c)	2.5×10^3 kg	-------	15 kN
d)	-------	0.6 m s^{-2}	10^4 N
e)	45 mg	-------	1.35 N
f)	75 tonnes	2×10^{-3} m s^{-2}	-------

51. A 9500 kg boat accelerates at 45 ×10⁻³ m s⁻². Calculate the unbalanced force.

52. A force of 16.3 N is applied to a mass of 50 g. Calculate the acceleration.

53. A force of 342 N on an object produces an acceleration of 3.8 m s⁻². What is the mass of the object?

54. Calculate the acceleration in the following:
   a) 5 N ← ☐ → 25 N, m = 4 kg
   b) 14 N ← ☐ → 36 N, m = 3 kg
   c) 8 N ← ☐ → 64 N, m = 7 kg

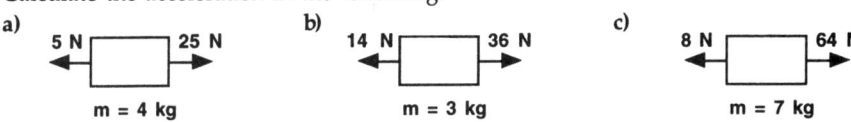

55. Calculate the acceleration in the following:
   a) 8 N ← ☐ → 9 N, ↓ 9 N, m = 200 g
   b) ↑ 3 N, 11 N ← ☐ → 29 N, ↓ 3 N, m = 9 kg
   c) 7 N ← ☐ → 14 N, ↓ 9 N, m = 4 kg

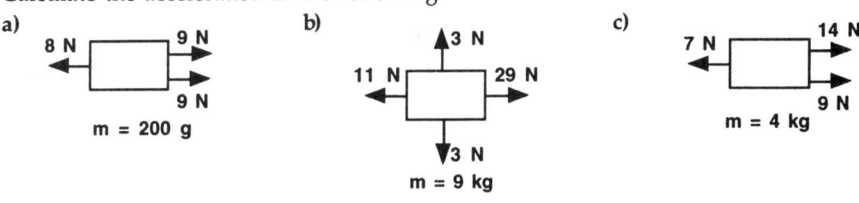

56. A force of 10⁻² N gives an acceleration of 87 m s⁻². What is the mass?

57. A trolley of mass 3.2 kg is pulled by a force of 17.5 N but there are frictional forces of 2.3 N acting. What is the acceleration of the trolley?

58. A car has a mass of 750 kg and the engine force acting is 2.5 kN. If the frictional force is 625 N, calculate the acceleration.

59. A toy bus of mass 375 g is accelerating at 2 m s⁻². If the frictional force acting is 1.3 N, calculate the applied force?

60. A trolley of mass 6.75 kg is accelerating at 3 m s⁻². If the frictional force acting is 3.75 N, what is the applied force?

61. If the frictional force acting on an object is 3.4 kN and the applied force is 7.3 kN, an acceleration of 0.75 m s⁻² is produced. What is its mass?

62. If the frictional force acting on an object is 0.54 N and the applied force is 0.66 N, an acceleration of 2.4 m s⁻² is produced. What is its mass?

63. An elastic applies an average force of 1.5 N to a mass of 0.6 kg and produces an acceleration of 2 m s⁻².
   a) What is the frictional force acting?
   b) If a second identical elastic is added to the first acting in the same direction, friction remaining constant, what is the resultant force acting?
   c) What is the new acceleration?

Standard Grade Physics

64. A force of 40 N is applied to a mass of 5 kg and produces an acceleration of 6 m s^{-2}.
   a) What is the frictional force acting?
   b) If a second identical force is added to the first in the same direction, friction remaining constant, what is the resultant force acting?
   c) What is the new acceleration?

65. A car has a mass of 600 kg while unladen. The driver has a mass of 70 kg and the engine produces a maximum acceleration of 2.4 m s^{-2}.
   a) What is the maximum force exerted by the engine?
   b) The car now picks up three more people and their luggage. The people average 70 kg each. The maximum force can now only produce an acceleration of 1.67 m s^{-2}.
      i) Calculate the total mass of the laden car.
      ii) Calculate the mass of the luggage.

66. A trolley has a mass of 4 kg and a resultant force of 18 N is applied to it.
   a) What is the acceleration produced?
   b) What is the speed after 6 s, starting from rest?

67. A rocket taking off from Earth has a mass of 4.5×10^3 kg and the engine force applied is 1×10^5 N.
   a) What is the resultant force acting?
   b) What is the acceleration produced?
   c) What is the speed achieved after 5 s, starting from rest?

68. A balloon has a mass of 700 kg and the buoyancy force is 8400 N.
   a) What is the resultant force acting?
   b) What is the acceleration produced?
   c) How long does it take to reach a speed of 12 m s^{-1}, starting from rest?

69. The ball has a resultant force of 6 N acting on it between **A** and **B** as shown. It takes 4 s to reach **B**. Between **B** and **C** there is a frictional force acting and the ball comes to a stop at **C** after a further 3 s.

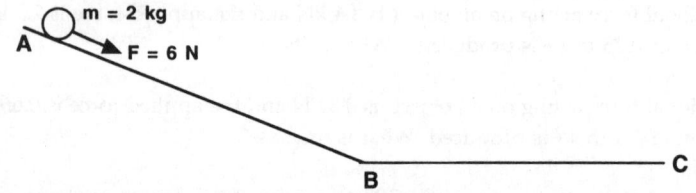

a) Calculate the acceleration between **A** and **B**.
b) Calculate the final speed at **B**, if the ball starts at rest.
c) Calculate the deceleration between **B** and **C**.
d) Calculate the frictional force acting.

70. A car of mass 750 kg starts from rest and accelerates at 5 m s^{-2} for 4 s. It continues at a constant speed for the next 6 s and then decelerates to rest in a further 8 s.
    a) Calculate the speed after 4 s.
    b) Draw a speed-time graph for the motion.
    c) Calculate the resultant force acting over the first 4 s.
    d) What is the resultant force between 4 and 10 s?
    e) Calculate the acceleration over the last 8 s.
    f) What is the unbalanced force acting during the last 8 s?
    g) What is the total distance travelled?
    h) What is the average speed?

71. A lorry of mass 2500 kg starts from rest and accelerates at 3.5 m s^{-2} for 6 s. It continues at a constant speed for the next 12 s and then decelerates to rest in a further 14 s.
    a) Calculate the speed after 6 s.
    b) Draw a speed-time graph for the motion.
    c) Calculate the resultant force acting over the first 6 s.
    d) What is the resultant force between 6 and 18 s?
    e) Calculate the acceleration over the last 14 s.
    f) What is the unbalanced force acting during the last 14 s?
    g) What is the total distance travelled?
    h) What is the average speed?

72. A boy picks up a large packing case which has a mass of 80 kg. It starts from rest and reaches a final speed of 0.5 m s^{-1} after 0.8 s. He then continues to lift it at a steady speed of 0.5 m s^{-1}.
    a) What is the initial acceleration of the box?
    b) What is the resultant force on the box while it is accelerating?
    c) What force does the boy have to exert while it is accelerating?
    d) What force does the boy exert when it is moving at a constant speed?

73. A weight-lifter lifts 250 kg at a constant speed of 1.5 m s^{-1}.
    a) What is the minimum force the weight-lifter must exert?
    b) Why must he be able to exert more force than this in practice?

74. a) A rocket has an initial mass of 3 x 10^4 kg and accelerates at 8 m s^{-2}.
        i) What is the resultant force on the rocket?
        ii) What is the force exerted by the engine?
    b) Sometime later, the engine is still producing the same force but fuel has been burnt and the mass has dropped to 2 x 10^4 kg.
        i) What is the new resultant force (assume *g* is still 10 N kg^{-1})?
        ii) What is the new acceleration?

75. A rocket has an initial mass of 5 x 10^3 kg and accelerates at 6 m s^{-2}. Sometime later, the engine is still producing the same force but the mass has dropped to 2 x 10^3 kg. What is the new acceleration?

Standard Grade Physics

WORK DONE $E_w = Fd$

76. Complete the following the table:

	FORCE	DISTANCE	WORK DONE
a)	80 N	5 m	-------
b)	------	32 m	608 J
c)	48 N	-------	36 J
d)	27 kN	95 cm	-------
e)	------	23 km	21.85 MJ
f)	666 N	-------	3×10^5 kJ

77. A man exerts a force of 2 kN on a wheelbarrow and pushes it for 150 m. How much work does he do?

78. A man exerts a force of 2 kN on a rock but fails to move it. How much work does he do?

79. A woman does 30 000 J of work in moving a lawn mower 150 m. What average force does she exert?

80. A man has to exert an average force of 260 N to push a trolley round a supermarket. If he does 208 kJ of work how far does he walk?

81. How much energy is used up by a car engine which exerts an average force of 3620 N for a distance of 5.7 km?

82. A trolley is brought to rest by a 7.5 N frictional force in a distance of 22.5 m. How much work is done by the frictional force?

83. A ship of mass 3500 tonnes is slowed by its engines (1 tonne = 1000 kg). It takes 6.8 km for the ship to stop and the engines exert a force of 70 kN. How much work do the engines do?

84. An ant has to do 2×10^{-3} J of work in dragging a leaf 175 cm. What force does the ant exert?

85. A man has to overcome a frictional force of 85 N and provide a resultant force of 226 N to move an object. If he moves the object a distance of 75 m, what is the work done?

86. There is a frictional force of 900 N acting on a car and the resultant force is 3600 N. If the car travels 2 km, what is the work done by the car's engine?

POTENTIAL ENERGY $E_p = mgh$

(Assume g is 10 N kg^{-1}.)

87. Copy and complete the following table:

	MASS	HEIGHT	POTENTIAL ENERGY
a)	5 kg	6 m	-------
b)	-------	120 m	5760 J
c)	19 kg	------	722 J
d)	600 g	------	0.9 J
e)	-------	750 cm	56.25 J
f)	5 tonnes	120 m	-------

88. A football of mass 2.5 kg is lifted to the top of a cliff. If the cliff is 180 m high, how much potential energy does the football gain?

89. A fly has a mass of 2.5 mg and flies up to a ceiling 3.5 m high. How much potential energy does the fly gain?

90. If a 30 kg boy gains 37 500 J of potential energy, how high is the cliff that he has climbed?

91. A box has a mass of 5.8 kg and is lifted onto a shelf in the garage from the floor. If it has gained 145 J of potential energy, how high is the shelf?

92. What is the mass of a ball which has 8.75 J of potential energy when it is 1.25 m in the air?

93. What is the mass of a model plane which has 2250 J of potential energy when it is 60 m in the air?

94. An object has a weight of 570 N and is lifted onto a shelf 2.75 m high. Calculate the gain in potential energy?

95. If a man weighing 630 N and climbs on a wall where he gains 2268 J of potential energy, how high is the wall?

96. A 500 g ball is pulled up a slope as shown. Calculate the potential energy it gains.

97. A 2.3 kg ball is pulled up a slope as shown. Calculate the potential energy it gains.

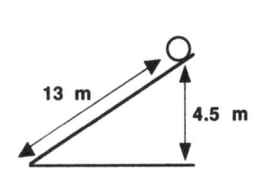

Standard Grade Physics

KINETIC ENERGY $E_k = \frac{1}{2} m v^2$

98. Complete the following table:

	MASS	VELOCITY	KINETIC ENERGY
a)	3 kg	6 m s^{-1}	--------
b)	--------	12 m s^{-1}	432 J
c)	8 kg	--------	100 J
d)	500 g	--------	30.25 J
e)	--------	15 m s^{-1}	2700 J
f)	12 kg	1.6 m s^{-1}	--------

99. How much kinetic energy has a 160 g cricket ball when it is thrown at 22 m s^{-1}?

100. How much kinetic energy has a 9000 kg plane when flying at 200 m s^{-1}?

101. What is the mass of a trolley, which has 141.75 J of kinetic energy, when it is travelling at 8 m s^{-1}?

102. What is the mass of a ball, which has 22.5 J of kinetic energy, when it is travelling at 7.5 m s^{-1}?

103. How fast is a 4 kg trolley moving, if it has 180.5 J of kinetic energy?

104. How fast is a 36 g toy car moving, if it has 40.5 mJ of kinetic energy?

105. A car of mass 900 kg accelerates at 2.5 m s^{-2} for 8 s from rest.
    a) How fast is the car travelling after 8 s.
    b) How much kinetic energy does the car have after 8 s?
    c) Where has this energy come from?

106. A car of mass 850 kg accelerates at 1.8 m s^{-2} for 5 s from 12 m s^{-1}.
    a) How fast is the car travelling after 5 s?
    b) How much kinetic energy does the car have at the start?
    c) How much kinetic energy does the car have after 5 s?
    d) How much kinetic energy has it gained during the 5 s?

107. A rocket of mass 1.5 x 10^4 kg accelerates at 220 m s^{-2} for 29 s from 5200 m s^{-1}.
    a) How fast is the rocket travelling after the 29 s?
    b) How much kinetic energy has it gained?
    c) If the rocket is in space and the engine is then switched off what will happen to its speed? Explain your answer.

ENERGY AND POWER $E = Pt$, $P = \dfrac{E}{t}$

108. Complete the following table (also see page 17):

	POWER	TIME	ENERGY
a)	825 W	17.5 s	-------
b)	-------	5 ms	3.2 J
c)	10^4 W	-------	3.6×10^7 J
d)	-------	1 h 25 mins	15.3 J
e)	4 mW	10^5 s	-------
f)	3.2 MW	-------	5.6×10^8 J

109. A cat takes 15 s to push a ball for 8.7 m with an average force of 1.9 N.
  a) How much work does the cat do?
  b) What power does the cat develop?

110. A lift motor has to move the fully laden lift 4 m between floors in 1.5 s. The fully laden lift has a mass of 1850 kg (friction can be ignored).
  a) Calculate the weight of the fully laden lift.
  b) What is the upward force in the cable when the lift is moving at a constant speed?
  c) What is the work done by the motor?
  d) What is the minimum power of the motor to lift it at a steady speed?

111. A motorised car with a mass of 1.4 kg travels up a long slope in 9.7 s. It gains a total vertical height of 0.8 m.
  a) What is the potential energy gained by the car?
  b) What is the power of the car?

112. A 60 kg pupil runs up a flight of stairs in 6.3 s. Each stair is 0.18 m high and there are 50 stairs in the flight.
  a) What is the total vertical height climbed?
  b) What is the potential energy gained by the pupil?
  c) What is the power developed by the pupil?

113. A girl can run 100 m in 12.5 s. She has a mass of 49 kg.
  a) Calculate her average speed.
  b) Calculate her kinetic energy, when running at a speed equal to her average speed.
  c) Calculate the average power developed during the run.

114. A car with a mass of 950 kg travels 4 km in 3.5 min at a constant speed.
  a) Calculate the constant speed of the car in metres per second.
  b) Calculate the kinetic energy of the car.
  c) Calculate the average power of the car.

POTENTIAL AND KINETIC ENERGY $E_p = E_k \Rightarrow v = \sqrt{(2gh)}$

115. A 1.3 kg ball is dropped from the top of a cliff which is 80 m high.
   a) Calculate the potential energy at the top of the cliff.
   b) State the kinetic energy at the bottom of the cliff, assuming that there is no friction.
   c) Calculate the speed of the ball at the bottom of the cliff.
   d) Which piece of information given in the question is not required to find the speed?

116. A box is dropped from a bridge 8.45 m high.
   a) Calculate the speed of the box just before it hits the ground.
   b) What assumption about energy has to be made to do this calculation?

117. A ball rolls off a table and hits the floor at 5 m s^{-1}. Calculate the height of the table.

118. A lump of ice falls off an aeroplane as it comes into land. If the ice hits the ground with a vertical speed of 85 m s^{-1} and friction can be ignored, what was the height of the plane?

119. A ball bearing rolls down a curtain track as shown (assume friction between the track and the ball can be ignored).

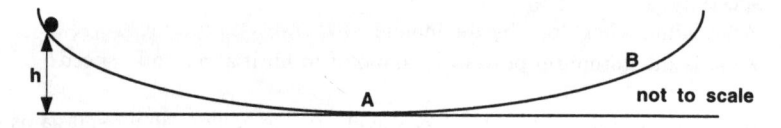

   a) i) Calculate the speed at **A**, if **h** is 115.2 cm,
      ii) Calculate the height of point **B**, the highest point reached.
      iii) Calculate the height at which the ball bearing would have to be placed for it to be travelling at 4 m s^{-1} at **A**.
   d) Suggest a method for measuring the speed at **A**.

120. A car of mass 900 kg is travelling at 30 m s^{-1}. At the bottom of a hill the driver switches off the engine and coasts up the hill until the car comes to a stop just at the top of the hill.
   a) What is the kinetic energy of the car at the bottom of the hill?
   b) What is the kinetic energy of the car at the top of the hill?
   c) What is the gain in potential energy of the car from the bottom to the top of the hill?
   d) What is the maximum vertical height the car can go up the hill?
   e) Why in practice will the actual vertical height be less than this?

121. A crane drops a girder from a height of 120 m.
   a) Calculate the maximum speed of the girder as it hits the ground?
   b) Why in practice will the speed be less than this?

GENERAL PROBLEMS

122. An escalator has a maximum power available of 3.5 kW. Assume that people have an average mass of 65 kg and have to be raised through a height of 8.5 m.
    a) Calculate how much energy is used by the escalator in 1 min.
    b) Calculate how much potential energy is gained by each person.
    c) Calculate the maximum number of people that can be moved in 1 min by the escalator.

123. A 2.5 kg trolley is pulled from rest by a force of 15 N. The frictional force acting is 3 N.
    a) What is the acceleration of the trolley?
    b) If the force acts for 8 s, what is the final speed of the trolley?
    c) How much kinetic energy does the trolley have after 8 s?
    d) After the 8 s the trolley moves onto a different surface and the applied force is removed. The trolley comes to a stop in 8 m.
        i) How much work is done by friction in stopping the trolley?
        ii) What is the frictional force on the new surface?

124. A 500 g ball is thrown vertically upwards at 20 m s^{-1}.
    a) How much kinetic energy does it have at the instant it leaves the hand?
    b) How much potential energy does it have at the top of the flight?
    c) How high does the ball go?
    d) How fast is the ball travelling when it is caught again (assume it is caught at the same height it was released from)?

125. A plane leaves the deck of an aircraft carrier with a speed of 120 m s^{-1}, just enough to get airborne. The plane has a mass of 30 000 kg.
    a) What is the minimum kinetic energy of the plane at take off?
    b) If he plane has 75 m in which to take off, what must be the average force acting on the plane in order for it to reach the correct speed?
    c) If the plane's engine can only supply 2 500 000 N, how much extra force has to be supplied?
    d) This force is supplied by a steam catapult which acts for 0.2 s.
        i) How much work is done by the steam catapult?
        ii) Calculate the power of the steam catapult.

126. A motor winch is used to lift a 50 kg bag of cement from the ground floor of a partially built block of flats up to the top floor. The vertical height is 92 m.
    a) How much potential energy does the cement gain?
    b) What is the minimum force the winch has to apply to lift the cement at a constant speed?
    c) How much work is done by the winch on the cement?
    d) If the winch has a power of 3.5 kW, calculate the minimum time it will it take to lift the cement?

Standard Grade Physics

127. The graph relates to a man's journey to work in his car.

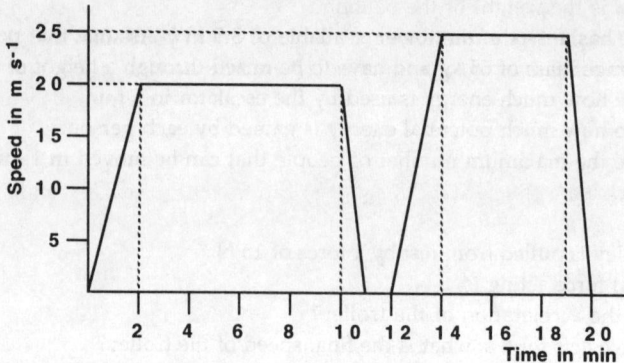

a) When is the man stopped at traffic lights?
b) Calculate the acceleration in metres per second in the first 2 min.
c) If the total mass of the man and the car is 1170 kg, what is the minimum force exerted by the car's engine?
d) What is the maximum kinetic energy of the car during the journey?
e) How far away does the man work?

128. A stunt man rides a motorbike off the edge of a cliff and lands it on a bridge 30 m below. He leaves the cliff top at 14 m s^{-1}. The bike and man have a total mass of 190 kg.
a) What is the kinetic energy of the man and bike on the cliff?
b) What is the potential energy of the man and bike on the cliff?
c) What is the maximum kinetic energy of the man and bike on the bridge (assume no energy is lost to other forms)?
d) What would the maximum speed be on the bridge?
e) In fact the bike is only travelling at 20 m s^{-1} as friction had been deliberately increased.
   i) How much kinetic energy does the bike actually have?
   ii) How much energy is lost due to friction?
   iii) What is the average force due to friction?

129. A skier is pulled up a slope by a ski tow and then skies back down. The skier has a mass of 65 kg and the slope is 3.6 km long and rises a vertical height of 1.8 km. The ski tow exerts an average force of 250 N on the skier and takes 15 min to pull him up.
a) How much work is done by the ski tow on the skier?
b) What is the minimum power the motor must have to pull up the one skier only?
c) How much potential energy does the skier gain?
d) What is the maximum kinetic energy at the bottom of the run if the skier just glides down the slope?
e) What is the maximum speed at the bottom of the run?
f) Why in practice would the actual speed be less than this?

130. a) A balloon has a total mass of 110 kg and it is hovering motionless in the air.
   i) What is the weight of the balloon?
   ii) What is the size of the buoyancy force? Explain your answer.
   b) The balloonist throws out 7.5 kg of ballast in order to rise.
   i) If the buoyancy force remains constant, find the acceleration of the balloon.
   ii) Calculate its vertical speed after 15 s.

131. Two cyclists have a competition to see who can travel furthest in 1 min. The graphs of their journeys are shown.

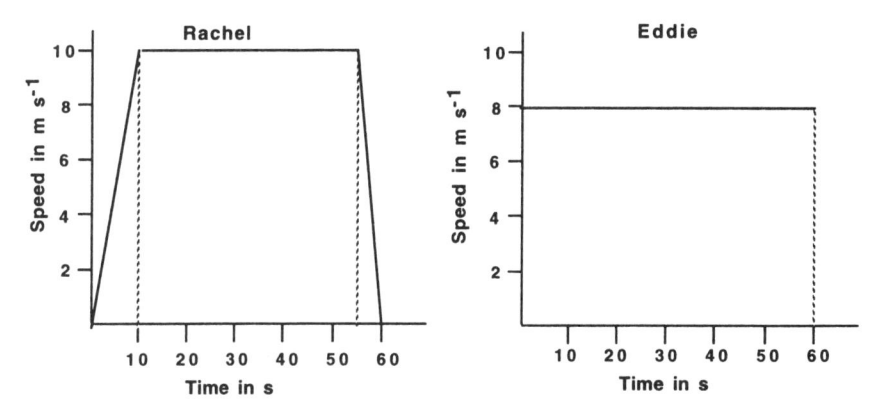

a) How far does Eddie travel in the minute?
b) How far does Rachel travel?
c) What is Rachel's acceleration over the first 10 s?
d) If the total mass of Rachel and her bike is 78 kg, what net force must she exert over the first 10 s?
e) Calculate the maximum kinetic energy of Rachel and her bike?
f) What force do the brakes exert on Rachel's bike to bring her to a stop over the last 5 s?

132. Two men are trying to push start a car of mass 900 kg. Each man can exert an average force of 340 N. The car needs an acceleration of 1.4 m s^{-2} in order to reach the speed required to start The frictional force is 90 N.
   a) What is the acceleration produced by the two men?
   b) When the car still does not start they call in two more men and all four push, still with the same average force.
   i) Calculate the acceleration now.
   ii) Does the car start?

133. A spider of mass 30 mg can climb vertically up a silk thread 2.8 m in 3.2 s.
   a) What is its average speed?
   b) What minimum force must it exert?
   c) What power does it develop?

Standard Grade Physics

ENERGY

SOURCES OF ENERGY

1. Name three fossil fuels.

2. Draw a table sorting the following into renewable and non-renewable sources of energy: solar; coal; wind; waves; peat; uranium; hydroelectric; gas; geothermal; oil; tidal.

3. Give the number of joules in:
   a) 1 MJ,
   b) 1 GJ,
   c) 500 kJ,
   d) 450 GJ.

4. A wind generator produces 400 kW of electrical power.
   a) What would be the total output power of 120 such generators?
   b) How much energy will be produced in 1 hour from the 120 generators?

5. 1 km of wave generators produces 3 GJ of electrical energy per day.
   a) How much electrical energy is produced by 4 km of wave generators?
   b) How much electrical energy is produced by the 4 km of wave generators per week?

6. A power station has an output power of 640 MW.
   How much electrical energy does it produce in 1 min?

7. A set of wave generators produce 8 GJ of energy in one day.
   Calculate the output power of the set of generators.

8. The electrical power requirement of the United Kingdom is 95 GW.
   a) How much electrical energy is used in 1 day?
   b) If a power station produces 400 MW, what percentage of the total requirement does it give?

9. One wave generator produces 250 kW of power.
   a) How much power would be produced by eight such generators?
   b) How many of these generators are required to give the same output as a coal fired power station giving 180 MW?

10. An electricity company produces 10 GW of power. If 0.5% of this power is produced from the wind, how much does the wind power contribute?

11. A wind generator gives 4 MW of power and requires 0.3 km^2 of space.
    a) How many generators are required to produce 80 MW?
    b) What total area would they occupy?

POWER STATIONS

12. A power station has an output power of 1.5×10^3 MW.
    a) How many joules are produced in 1 s?
    b) How many joules are produced in 1 h?

13. In a coal fired power station each kilogram of coal gives 28 MJ of energy.
    a) How many kilograms of coal are required each second for a 252 MW power station?
    b) How many kilograms of coal will the station use in 1 h?
    c) How many kilograms of coal will the station use in 1 day?

14. A coal fired power station produces 800 MW of electrical power at 400 kV. Calculate the current that the power station delivers.

15. A nuclear power station produces 1.3 GW of electrical power at 400 kV. Calculate the current that the power station delivers.

16. A power station produce electrical power at 400 kV and 2.3 kA. What is its output power?

17. A power station produce electrical power at 430 kV and 3.1 kA. What is its output power?

18. How long does it take a 250 MW power station to produce 30 GJ of energy?

19. Calculate how long it takes to produce 100 GJ of energy from:
    a) an 800 MW coal fired power station,
    b) a 1.3 GW nuclear power station.

20. 1 kg of gas produces 37 MJ of heat.
    How many kilograms are required each second for a 750 MW power station?

21. 1 kg of coal produces 28 MJ of heat.
    How many kilograms are required each second for a 750 MW power station?

22. 1 kg of oil produces 44 MJ of heat.
    How many kilograms are required each second for a 750 MW power station?

23. 1 kg of nuclear fuel produces 2.1×10^{12} J of heat.
    What mass of fuel is needed to produce 6.0×10^{13} J of heat?

24. A nuclear power station uses 2100 MJ of heat energy per second. 1 kg of nuclear fuel produces 2.1×10^{12} J of heat.
    a) For how long will the kilogram of fuel last?
    b) How many kilograms are required for 24 h?

Standard Grade Physics

EFFICIENCY

$$\%Efficiency = \frac{E_{out}}{E_{in}} \times 100\% = \frac{P_{out}}{P_{in}} \times 100\%$$

25. Complete the following table:

	P_{in}	P_{out}	Efficiency
a)	100 W	75 W	--------
b)	--------	360 W	50%
c)	850 W	--------	40 %
d)	--------	630 MW	42%
e)	1420 MW	860 MW	--------
f)	1.6×10^6 W	--------	39%

26. What is the efficiency of a bulb which uses 540 J of electrical energy and gives out 108 J of light?

27. A power station uses up 250 MJ of chemical energy to produce 105 MJ of electrical energy. How efficient is the power station?

28. An oil fired power station produces 1.7 GW of heat, which gives 630 MW of electrical power. Calculate its efficiency.

29. A power station produces 1600 MW of heat, which gives 600 MW of electrical power. Calculate its efficiency.

30. A power station is 35% efficient.
    How much useful energy is produced when 145 MJ of energy are used up?

31. Give two reasons why:
    a) a hydroelectric power station is not 100% efficient,
    b) a coal fired power station is not 100% efficient.

32. A power station is 42% efficient.
    How much chemical energy has to be put in to get 230 MJ of electrical energy out?

33. An oil fired power station has to use up 348 MJ of chemical energy to generate 194 MJ of electrical energy.
    a) How much energy has been 'lost'?
    b) Suggest where the lost energy has gone.

34. A power station produces 800 MW of electrical power.
    How much power must be put in if the power station is 32% efficient?

35. A power station is 41% efficient. If it produces 500 MJ of electrical energy per second, what is the input power to the station?

36. A coal fired power station needs 260 MJ of heat per second. 1 kg of coal produces 2.8×10^7 J of heat.
   a) For how long will 1 kg of coal last?
   b) How many kilograms are required for 24 h?

37. A solar cell converts 8% of the sunlight falling on it into electricity.
   a) If the sunlight provides 2 kW m^{-2} and the solar cell has an area of 7.5 m^2, how much electrical power is produced?
   b) How many square metres of solar cell are required to give an output equivalent to a 750 MW coal fired power station?

38. A wind powered generator requires 8×10^6 J of energy every second to produce 3 MW of electricity. Calculate the efficiency of the aero-generator.

39. A coal fired power station generates 2.3×10^3 A of electricity at 400 kV.
   a) What is the output power from the power station?
   b) If the efficiency of the power station is 39%, how much chemical energy has to be provided by the coal every second?
   c) If 1 kg of coal produces 28 MJ of energy, how many kilograms are required every second?

40. An oil fired power station generates 3.2×10^3 A of electricity at 400 kV.
   a) What is the output power from the power station?
   b) If the efficiency of the power station is 41%, how much chemical energy has to be provided by the oil every second?
   c) If 1 kg of oil produces 44 MJ of energy, how many kilograms are required every second?

41. An area equivalent to 40 m by 60 m is covered by solar cells. Sunlight provides 2 kW m^{-2}.
   a) How much energy is collected by all the solar cells per second?
   b) If the output power is 576 kW, calculate the efficiency of the solar cells.

ENERGY CONVERSIONS

42. Give the main energy conversion in the following:
    a) a ball falling
    b) a working motor
    c) a bicycle dynamo
    d) a coal fire burning
    e) a battery driven toy car
    f) an arrow fired from a bow
    g) a moving diesel train

43. A boy drops a 1.5 kg stone off the top of a cliff, which is 180 m high.
    a) How much potential energy does the stone have at the top, relative to the foot of the cliff?
    b) Ignoring friction, how much kinetic energy does it have just as it reaches the bottom?
    c) How fast is it travelling the instant before it hits the ground?

44. The following identical balls are moved from the bottom to the top as shown.

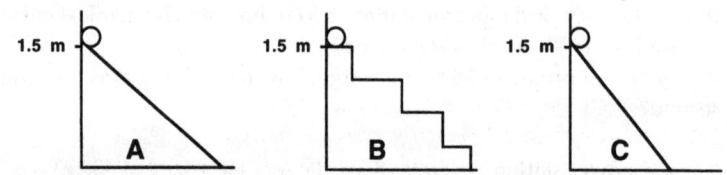

    1.5 m   A   1.5 m   B   1.5 m   C

    Which has the most potential energy?

45. A 12 V motor requires a current of 3 A to work correctly.
    a) What is the input power of the motor?
    b) How much energy does it use in 5 min?
    c) If it produces 8.64 kJ of heat energy, how much kinetic energy does it produce in the 5 min ignore any other possible forms of energy)?
    d) What is the efficiency of the motor?

46. A 3 kW kettle is used to heat 1.75 kg of water. It should take 6×10^5 J of energy to heat the water to boiling.
    a) How long should the kettle take to boil the water?
    b) The kettle actually takes 4 min 30 s to boil the water. How much energy does the kettle use?
    c) Calculate the efficiency of the kettle.

47. A dynamo gives a voltage of 24 V and a current of 3.5 A. The electrical energy produced is used to make a small model move.
    a) What is the output power of the dynamo?
    b) If the model produces 20 kJ of kinetic energy in 10 min, what is the efficiency of the system?

48. A model of a pumped storage system used a small pump to raise 4.5 litres of water through an average height of 2.8 m. It took 45 s for the water to be collected. The working pump had a voltage of 9.8 V and a current of 2 A while it was working.
   a) If 1 litre of water has a mass of 1 kg, what is the mass of water raised?
   b) How much potential energy is gained by the water?
   c) What is the electrical energy supplied to the pump?
   d) What is the efficiency of the system?
   e) What has happened to the 'lost' energy?

49. a) Describe what is meant by a pumped storage system.
    b) What are the advantages of a pumped storage system?
    c) When is the water pumped up to the reservoir?

50. A bus and a car start from rest at the bottom of a hill. Both reach the top of the hill moving at 12 m s^{-1}, having moved up 150 m vertically. The bus has a mass of 4500 kg and carries 19 passengers and a driver while the car has a mass of 700 kg and only contains the driver. Assume all the people have an average mass of 70 kg. Both the car and the bus use petrol which provides 20 MJ of energy for each kilogram. The car uses 0.3 kg of petrol and the bus uses 2.3 kg of petrol.
   a) i) Calculate the total mass of the car and driver.
      ii) Calculate the potential energy gained by the car.
      iii) Calculate the kinetic energy gained by the car.
      iv) Calculate the total energy gained by the car.
      v) How much energy is provided by the petrol used by the car?
      vi) Calculate the efficiency for the car.
   b) i) Calculate the total mass of the bus and people.
      ii) Calculate the potential energy gained by the bus.
      iii) Calculate the kinetic energy gained by the bus.
      iv) Calculate the total energy gained by the bus.
      v) How much energy is provided by the petrol used by the bus?
      vi) Calculate the efficiency for the bus.
   c) Calculate how much energy is required for each person on:
      i) the car,
      ii) the bus.

51. A dam stores 1.2 x 10^{10} kg of water and is 430 m above the turbine of a hydroelectric scheme.
   a) Calculate the potential energy of the water in the dam.
   b) If the pipe delivers 1280 kg of water to the turbine every second, how long would the water in the reservoir last, if there was no rain?
   c) How much potential energy is lost by the water every second?
   d) If the turbine is 55% efficient, what is the power output of the turbine?
   e) If this was a pumped storage system, what would be the minimum power required for the pump?

Standard Grade Physics

TRANSFORMERS $\dfrac{V_s}{V_p} = \dfrac{N_s}{N_p}$

(Assume 100% efficiency for all transformers.)

52. Complete the following table:

	V_p	N_p	V_s	N_s
a)	20 V	100	5 V	--------
b)	240 V	360	--------	12
c)	--------	500	8 V	125
d)	60 V	--------	240 V	800
e)	240 V	1000	3 kV	--------
f)	--------	2000	2.4 MV	3×10^4
g)	14 kV	--------	240 V	10^3
h)	400 kV	5×10^5	--------	13 750

53. a) For the following transformers, find the voltage in the secondary:

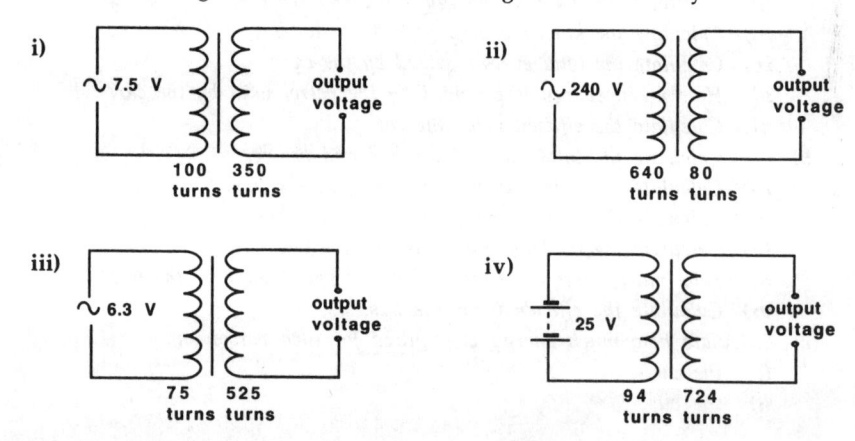

i) ~ 7.5 V, 100 turns, 350 turns, output voltage

ii) ~ 240 V, 640 turns, 80 turns, output voltage

iii) ~ 6.3 V, 75 turns, 525 turns, output voltage

iv) 25 V, 94 turns, 724 turns, output voltage

b) Which of the above circuits shows a step-up transformer?
c) Which of the above circuits shows a step-down transformer?

54. A mains supply is used with a transformer to provide 12 V for a model train set. If there are 356 turns on the secondary, how many are required for the primary?

55. A transformer with a turns ratio ($N_p : N_s$) of 25:1 is used to provide an output voltage of 3.6 V. What is the input voltage?

56. For the following transformers, find the missing number of turns:

a) 240 V primary, 11 kV secondary, Np = ?, 13 750 turns secondary.

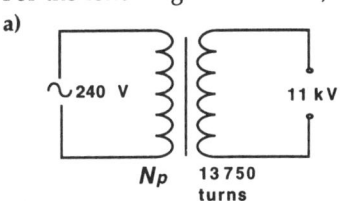

b) 22 V primary, 88 V secondary, 200 turns primary, Ns = ?

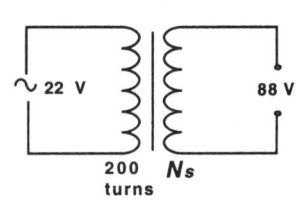

c) 24 V primary, 5.4 V secondary, 800 turns primary, Ns = ?

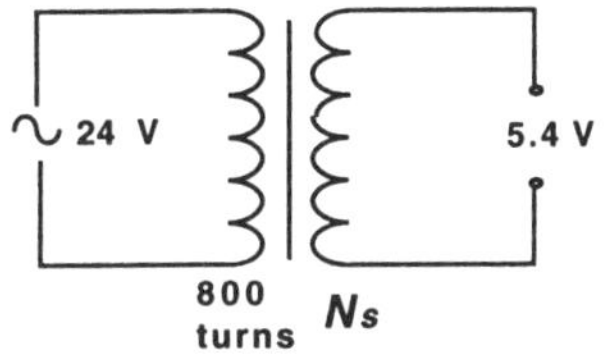

d) 75 V primary, 225 V secondary, Np = ?, 3360 turns secondary.

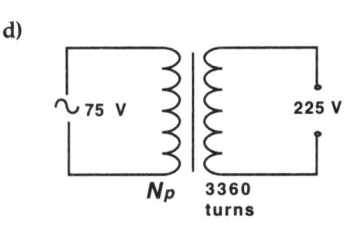

57. A mains transformer with 20 000 turns on the primary is used to power a 9.6 V toy train. How many turns are required on the secondary?

58. A transformer is used to change an input voltage of 11 kV to supply the mains voltage of a house. If there are 1.045×10^5 turns on the primary, how many are required on the secondary?

59. A transformer has an output voltage of 326 V.
If the turns ratio ($N_p : N_s$) is 1:8.15, what is the input voltage?

60. The output voltage required from a transformer, for part of a hi fi system, is 8 V. There are 375 turns on the primary and 12 000 turns on the secondary. What is the input voltage?

61. A transformer has 4500 turns on the secondary and 1350 turns on the primary. If the output voltage is 56 V, what is the input voltage?

62. A 12 W bulb is run at its correct rating from a transformer as shown.
   a) Calculate the output voltage across the bulb.
   b) Calculate the current through the bulb.
   c) Calculate the resistance of the bulb.

   (240 V primary, 2000 turns primary, 150 turns secondary, 12 W bulb)

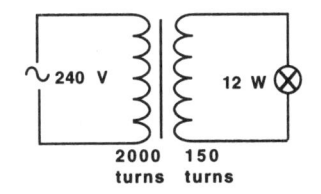

63. A 150 W bulb is run at its correct rating from a transformer as shown.
   a) Calculate the output voltage across the bulb.
   b) Calculate the current through the bulb.
   c) Calculate the resistance of the bulb.

   (240 V primary, 640 turns primary, 96 turns secondary, 150 W bulb)

Standard Grade Physics

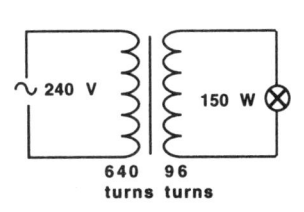

CURRENT IN TRANSFORMERS $\quad \dfrac{I_p}{I_s} = \dfrac{N_s}{N_p}$

64. Complete the following table:

	I_p	N_p	I_s	N_s
a)	2.5 A	100	5 A	--------
b)	0.5 A	360	--------	12
c)	--------	500	8 A	125
d)	0.6 A	--------	2.4 A	800
e)	2.4 A	120	300 mA	--------
f)	--------	2000	75 mA	3×10^4
g)	45 mA	--------	0.18 A	10^3
h)	300 µA	5×10^5	--------	13 750

65. For the following transformers, calculate the missing current:

a) I_p ; 2.8 A ; 245 turns ; 35 turns

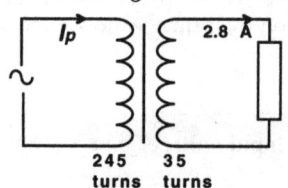

b) 6.9 A ; I_s ; 200 turns ; 1200 turns

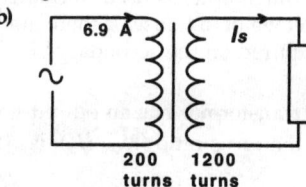

c) 1.2 A ; I_s ; 1750 turns ; 250 turns

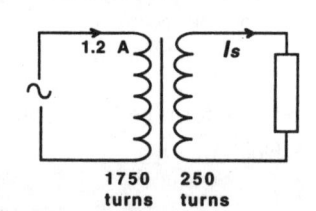

d) I_p ; 800 µA ; 1.2×10^2 turns ; 3×10^5 turns

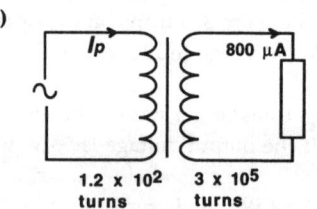

66. A transformer has currents of 7.5 A in the primary and 300 mA in the secondary.
   a) If there are 2000 turns on the primary, how many turns are there on the secondary?
   b) Is this a step-up or step-down transformer?

67. A transformer has currents of 50 mA in the primary and 2.5 A in the secondary.
   a) If there are 750 turns on the secondary, how many turns are there on the primary?
   b) Is this a step-up or step-down transformer?

COMPLETE TRANSFORMER EQUATION $\frac{V_s}{V_p} = \frac{N_s}{N_p} = \frac{I_p}{I_s}$

68. Complete the following table:

	V_p	N_p	I_p	V_s	N_s	I_s
a)	---i---	5000	---ii---	660 V	1×10^4	400 mA
b)	5 kV	980	60 mA	---i---	---ii---	0.24 A
c)	---i---	---ii---	8 A	56 V	336	2 A
d)	240 V	9600	1.5 A	20 V	---i---	---ii---
e)	39 V	380	5.2 A	---i---	4940	---ii---
f)	---i---	6480	---ii---	15 V	720	9.6 A

69. For the following transformers, calculate the missing current, voltage or number of turns (**two** in each diagram):

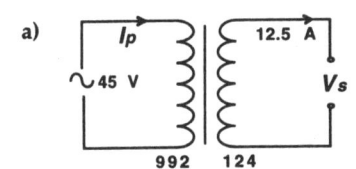

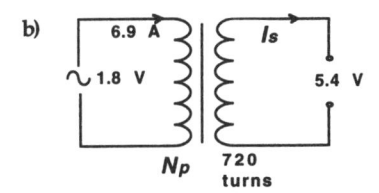

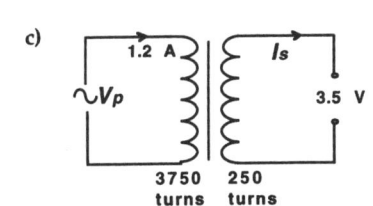

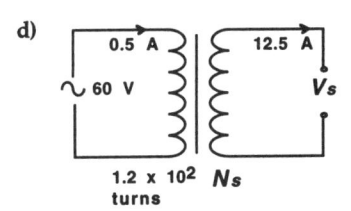

a) I_p, 45 V, 12.5 A, V_s, 992 turns, 124 turns

b) 6.9 A, 1.8 V, I_s, 5.4 V, N_p, 720 turns

c) 1.2 A, V_p, I_s, 3.5 V, 3750 turns, 250 turns

d) 0.5 A, 60 V, 12.5 A, V_s, 1.2×10^2 N_s turns

70. A transformer has a turns ratio ($N_p : N_s$) of 1 : 560 and an input voltage of 240 V.
   a) What is the output voltage?
   b) If the current in the primary is 3.5 A, what is the current in the secondary?

Standard Grade Physics

EFFICIENCY IN TRANSFORMERS

71. Calculate the output voltage and the efficiency:

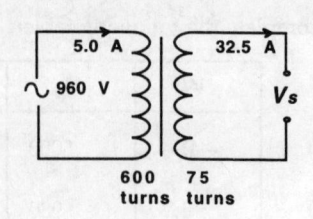

a) Primary: 1.0 A, 20 V, 600 turns; Secondary: 3.6 A, V_s, 150 turns

b) Primary: 5.0 A, 960 V, 600 turns; Secondary: 32.5 A, V_s, 75 turns

72. Calculate the efficiency and the voltage in the primary:

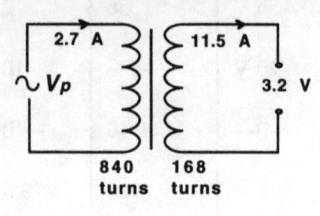

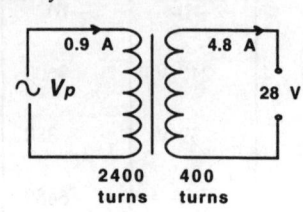

a) Primary: 2.7 A, V_p, 840 turns; Secondary: 11.5 A, 3.2 V, 168 turns

b) Primary: 0.9 A, V_p, 2400 turns; Secondary: 4.8 A, 28 V, 400 turns

73. Calculate the output current and the number of turns in the secondary:

a) Efficiency = 85%

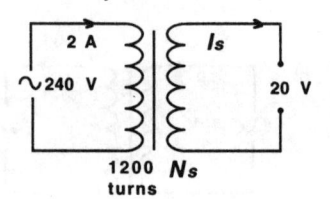

Primary: 2 A, 240 V, 1200 turns; Secondary: I_s, 20 V, N_s

b) Efficiency = 90%

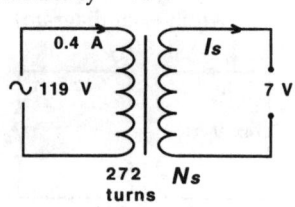

Primary: 0.4 A, 119 V, 272 turns; Secondary: I_s, 7 V, N_s

74. Calculate the output current and the number of turns in the primary:

a) Efficiency = 80%

Primary: 2.4 A, 720 V, N_p; Secondary: I_s, 180 V, 360 turns

b) Efficiency = 92%

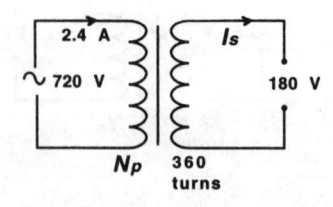

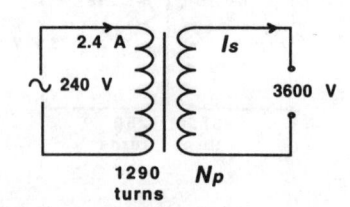

Primary: 2.4 A, 240 V, 1290 turns; Secondary: I_s, 3600 V, N_p

75. Calculate the current and voltage in the primary:

a) Efficiency = 75%

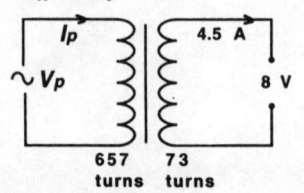

Primary: I_p, V_p, 657 turns; Secondary: 4.5 A, 8 V, 73 turns

b) Efficiency = 95%

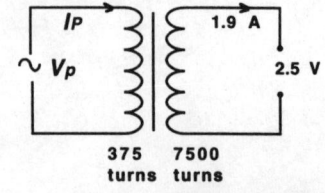

Primary: I_p, V_p, 375 turns; Secondary: 1.9 A, 2.5 V, 7500 turns

TRANSMISSION LINES (Assume 100% efficiency for all transformers.)

76.

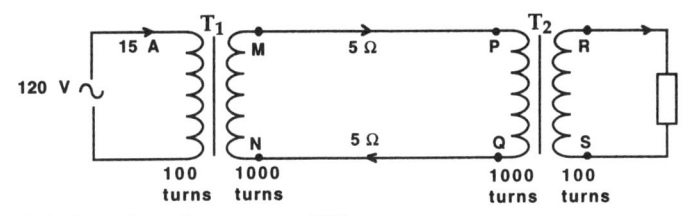

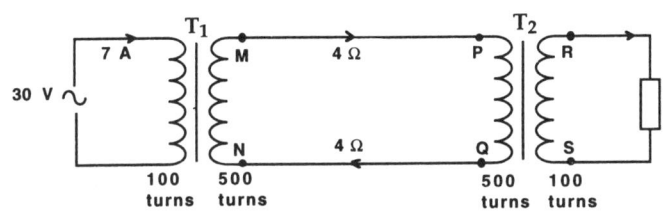

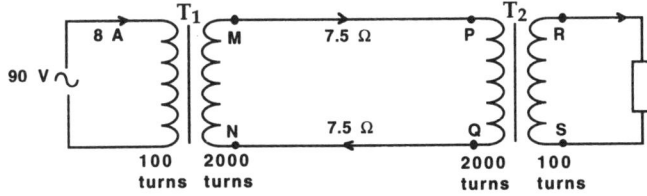

[Circuit diagram: 120 V AC source, 15 A, connected to T₁ (100 turns : 1000 turns) with M, N on secondary. Two 5 Ω transmission line resistors between MN and PQ. T₂ (1000 turns : 100 turns) with P, Q on primary and R, S on secondary connected to a resistor.]

a) Calculate the voltage across MN.
b) Calculate the current in MPQN.
c) Calculate the voltage across MP and QN.
d) Calculate the power loss in both transmission lines.
e) Calculate the voltage across PQ.
f) Calculate the voltage across RS.
g) Calculate the current through the resistor in the secondary of T_2.
h) What is the resistance of the resistor?

77.

[Circuit diagram: 30 V AC source, 7 A, connected to T₁ (100 turns : 500 turns) with M, N on secondary. Two 4 Ω transmission line resistors between MN and PQ. T₂ (500 turns : 100 turns) with P, Q on primary and R, S on secondary connected to a resistor.]

a) Calculate the voltage across MN.
b) Calculate the current in MPQN.
c) Calculate the voltage across MP and QN.
d) Calculate the power loss in both transmission lines.
e) Calculate the voltage across PQ.
f) Calculate the voltage across RS.
g) Calculate the current through the resistor in the secondary of T_2.
h) What is the resistance of the resistor?

78.

[Circuit diagram: 90 V AC source, 8 A, connected to T₁ (100 turns : 2000 turns) with M, N on secondary. Two 7.5 Ω transmission line resistors between MN and PQ. T₂ (2000 turns : 100 turns) with P, Q on primary and R, S on secondary connected to a resistor.]

a) Calculate the voltage across MN.
b) Calculate the current in MPQN.
c) Calculate the voltage across MP and QN.
d) Calculate the power loss in both transmission lines.
e) Calculate the voltage across PQ.
f) Calculate the voltage across RS.
g) Calculate the current through the resistor in the secondary of T_2.
h) What is the resistance of the resistor?

Standard Grade Physics

HEAT ENERGY   (no change of state) $E_h = c\, m\, \Delta T$

79. Complete the following table:

	c	m	ΔT	E_h
a)	4180 J kg^{-1} $^\circ$C^{-1}	2 kg	80 $^\circ$C	--------
b)	900 J kg^{-1} $^\circ$C^{-1}	1.5 kg	-------	337 500 J
c)	------	8 kg	120 $^\circ$C	384 000 J
d)	130 J kg^{-1} $^\circ$C^{-1}	--------	88 $^\circ$C	2860 J
e)	2100 J kg^{-1} $^\circ$C^{-1}	250 g	15 $^\circ$C	-------
f)	------	50 mg	65 $^\circ$C	7.5 J
g)	720 J kg^{-1} $^\circ$C^{-1}	--------	225 $^\circ$C	165 MJ
h)	3300 J kg^{-1} $^\circ$C^{-1}	800 g	-------	37 kJ

In the following questions assume there is no heat loss unless otherwise stated.
Use the following heat capacities:

    water   4180 J kg^{-1} $^\circ$C^{-1}
    methylated spirits   2300 J kg^{-1} $^\circ$C^{-1}
    aluminium   880 J kg^{-1} $^\circ$C^{-1}
    copper   380 J kg^{-1} $^\circ$C^{-1}
    lead   130 J kg^{-1} $^\circ$C^{-1}

80. Calculate the heat energy which is required to raise the temperature of:
    a) 4 kg of water from 10 $^\circ$C to 20 $^\circ$C,
    b) 100 g of aluminium from 100 $^\circ$C to 500 $^\circ$C,
    c) 1.5 kg of copper by 100 $^\circ$C,
    d) 50 g of lead from 50 $^\circ$C to 450 $^\circ$C.

81. Calculate the rise in temperature when 10 000 J are supplied to:
    a) 2 kg of water,
    b) 2.5 kg of aluminium,
    c) 600 g of copper,
    d) 1.5 kg of methylated spirits.

82. Calculate the mass of material which is present if 20 000 J of energy produces a rise in temperature of 20 $^\circ$C in:
    a) water,
    b) aluminium,
    c) copper,
    d) lead.

83. A 2 kW heater is used to heat a 3 kg block of aluminium for 3 min. What rise in temperature is produced?

84. 1 x 10^6 J of energy are supplied to 10 kg of copper at 20 °C.
   a) What will be the final temperature of the copper?
   b) The copper is now left to cool and loses heat at the rate of 4000 J s^{-1}. What will be its temperature after 1 min 40 s?

85. a) A kettle with a 2500 W element contains 1.5 kg of water. If the initial temperature of the water is 20 °C, how long will it take to bring the water to the boil, assuming all the heat goes into the water?
   b) How will the actual time compare with the time calculated. Explain your answer.

86. 300 g of water at 20 °C are contained in a copper can of mass 100 g. The temperature of both the water and the copper can is then raised to 40 °C by a 50 W immersion heater.
   a) What is the rise in temperature?
   b) How much heat is absorbed by the water?
   c) How much heat is absorbed by the copper?
   d) How much total heat is absorbed?
   e) How long does it take?

87. A heater is used to heat a 5 kg block of aluminium. The heater, operating from a 240 V supply, draws a current of 4 A. The heater is switched on for 2 min.
   a) How much electrical energy is supplied to the aluminium in this time?
   b) Hence calculate the maximum rise in temperature possible. State any assumptions clearly.

88. A kettle with a 2 kW element contains 1 kg of water initially at a temperature of 15 °C. Assume 80% of the heat produced by the kettle goes to heating the water.
   a) How much heat does the water need to absorb to rise to the boiling point?
   b) How much heat was supplied by the kettle in this time?
   c) How long does it take to heat the water to boiling?

89. A shower heater is rated at 7.5 kW and heats 3.2 kg of water for a shower. The water has to be heated from 15 °C to 40 °C.
   a) How much heat energy is required to heat the water?
   b) If the shower heater is on for 3 min, how much energy does it provide?
   c) What is the efficiency of the system?

Standard Grade Physics

90. In an experiment to find the specific heat capacity of copper the apparatus shown was used.

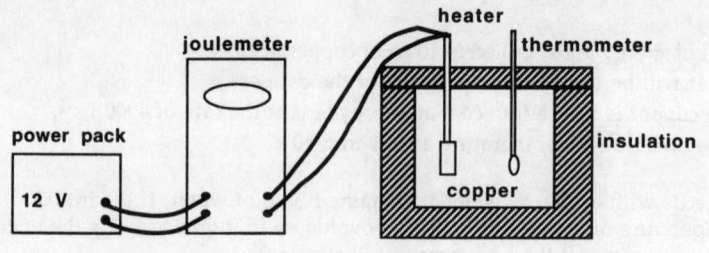

The following experimental results were obtained:
initial thermometer reading = 19 °C
final thermometer reading = 25 °C
initial joulemeter reading = 79 500 J
final joulemeter reading = 82 000 J
mass of copper block = 1 kg

a) What was the rise in temperature of the copper?
b) How much electrical energy was supplied?
c) Use these results to calculate the specific heat capacity of the copper.
d) The actual specific heat capacity of copper is 380 J kg^{-1} °C^{-1}. Account for the difference between this value and the experimental value calculated in part c).

91. The following experiment was set up to investigate heating a copper block.

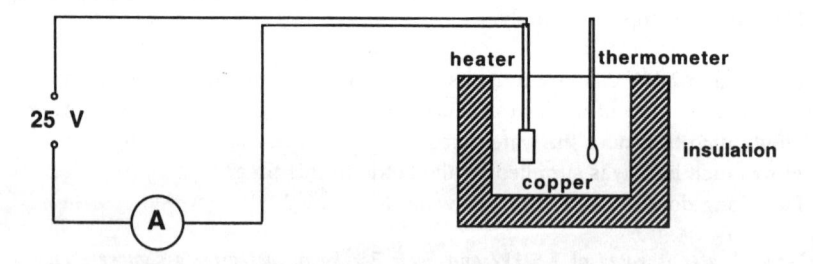

The following results were taken:
specific heat capacity of copper = 380 J kg^{-1} °C^{-1}
mass of copper = 650 g
temperature rise = 15 °C
time the heater was on = 71.2 s
voltage of the supply = 25 V

a) Use the above data to calculate the reading on the ammeter.
b) State clearly any assumptions made.
c) Calculate the power of the heater.

HEAT (with a change of state) $E_h = mL$

92. Complete the following table:

	m	L	E_h
a)	5 kg	2.26×10^6 J kg^{-1}	--------
b)	------	9.9×10^4 J kg^{-1}	35 640 J
c)	3 kg	--------	75 000 J
d)	------	8.3×10^5 J kg^{-1}	74.7 kJ
e)	375 g	--------	0.42 MJ
f)	20 mg	2.05×10^5 J kg^{-1}	--------

93. a) When changing state, the temperature of a substance remains constant even though energy is supplied. What happens to the energy supplied?
   b) What is meant by the specific latent heat of a substance?
   c) Explain the difference between the specific latent heat of fusion and the specific latent heat of vaporisation?
   d) Explain the difference between the specific latent heat (fusion or vaporisation) and the specific heat capacity of a substance?

Use the following information for Qs. 94 to 110.
specific heat capacities   water 4180 J kg^{-1} °C^{-1} ice 2100 J kg^{-1} °C^{-1}
specific latent heat of fusion of water 3.34×10^5 J kg^{-1}
specific latent heat of vaporisation of water 2.26×10^6 J kg^{-1}

94. How much energy is required to change 2.6 kg of ice at 0 °C into water at the same temperature?

95. How much energy is required to change 2.6 kg of water at 100 °C into steam at the same temperature?

96. You are given 4 kg of ice at 0 °C.
   a) How much energy is required to melt all the ice without raising the temperature?
   b) How much energy is required to bring the resulting water to boiling point?
   c) How much energy is required to change the water into steam at 100 °C?
   d) How much total energy is required to change 4 kg of ice at 0 °C into 4 kg of steam at 100 °C?

97. *How much energy is required in total to change 1.9 kg of ice at -10 °C to steam at 100 °C?*

Standard Grade Physics   93

98. 300 g of liquid ether are supplied with 2.8 x 10⁵ J of energy and turned into a vapour.
    a) Calculate the latent heat of vaporisation of ether.
    b) Explain whether the calculated answer is likely to be higher or lower than the true value.

99. The apparatus shown was used to find the specific latent heat of fusion of water.

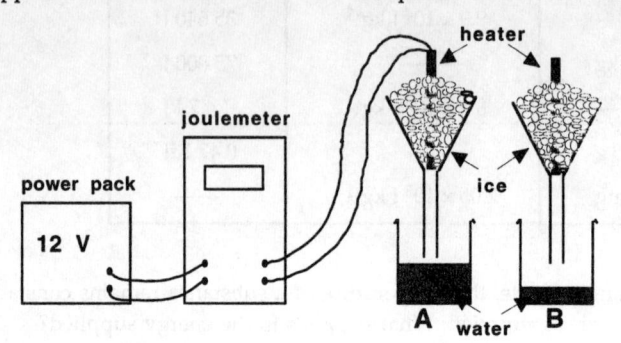

The following results were taken:
    mass of water in beaker **A**   = 0.1 kg
    mass of water in beaker **B**   = 0.02 kg
    initial reading on joulemeter   = 43 500 J
    final reading on joulemeter   = 71 500 J

    a) Why was the second heater and beaker B used?
    b) Calculate the specific latent heat of fusion of water.
    c) Explain why the answer does not agree with the accepted value.

100. An electric kettle has a power rating of 3 kW.
    a) How long should it take to bring 2 kg of water at an initial temperature of 20 °C to the boil.
    b) In practice it takes 4.5 min.
        i) How much energy is lost to surroundings?
        ii) What is the efficiency of the kettle?

101. A bath is approximately rectangular in shape, 1.5 m long and 0.6 m broad.
    a) Calculate the approximate volume of water in the bath when the water is 25 cm deep.
    b) Calculate the mass of this water given that 1 m³ of water has a mass of 1 x 10³ kg.
    c) Calculate the heat energy required to heat water from 20 °C for a hot bath (estimate the temperature required).
    d) Calculate the minimum time required to heat the water with a 4 kW heater.

TEMPERATURE - TIME GRAPHS

102. The following graph was obtained when heating a substance at a constant rate.

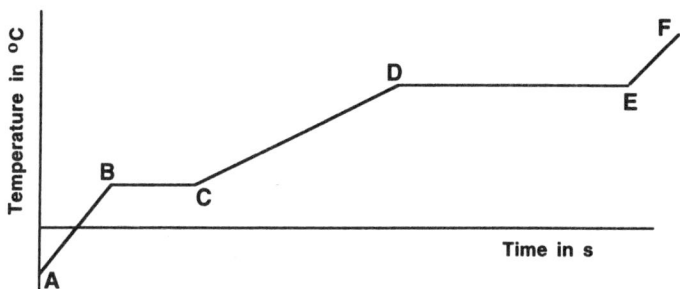

    a) Describe what is happening at each stage of the graph.
    b) Give the parts of the graph which correspond to:
       i) the melting point,
       ii) the boiling point of the substance.
    c) Why is **DE** longer than **BC**?
    d) Which part indicates the highest specific heat capacity?

103. The following graph was obtained when heating 125 g of a liquid with a 50 W heater.

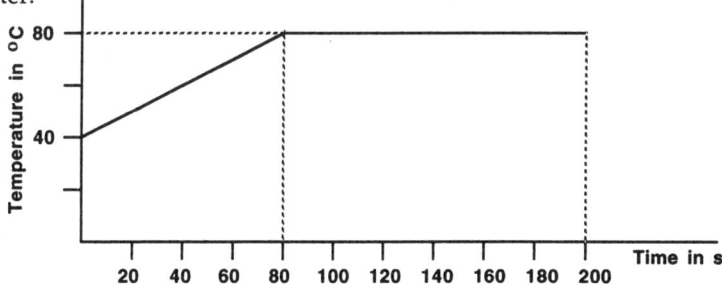

    a) Calculate the specific heat capacity of the liquid.
    b) Calculate the specific latent heat of vaporisation.

104. 0.2 kg of ice at -20 °C is heated by a 3 kW heater until it all turns to steam at 100 °C.
    a) Calculate the energy required for each stage and thus the total energy needed.
    b) Calculate the time needed for each stage, assuming no energy losses.
    c) Use the above answers to draw a temperature - time graph.

Standard Grade Physics

MIXED PROBLEMS ON HEAT

105. In a refrigerator, a pump is continually causing 120 g of liquid to evaporate and then condense for every stroke it makes.
   a) i) Where does the evaporation take place?
      ii) Where does the condensation take place?
   b) If the specific latent heat of vaporisation of the liquid is 2.5×10^5 J kg^{-1}, calculate how much heat energy is removed by each stroke.
   c) If there are 40 strokes per minute, how much energy is removed per second?

106. Ice cubes, each of which has a mass of 30 g, are used to cool a drink. If the freezer is set at -8 °C, how much heat energy will one ice cube remove from a drink as it melts completely?

107. A house is heated by radiators. In order to cut down heat loss, foil is placed behind the radiators.
   a) How does the foil help?
   b) What materials could be used to help stop heat loss through the roof?

108. A warehouse is used to store apples over winter. It is important that the apples do not freeze or the fruit would spoil. Some barrels of water are placed among the crates of apples .
   a) If 12 barrels each containing 70 kg of water freeze when the temperature drops to -8 °C overnight, how much heat energy is released?
   b) What is the advantage of this?

109. Marie has a mass of 70 kg and eats enough food each day to supply her with 14 MJ of energy.
   a) If all this energy was given to 70 kg of water at body temperature, what would the final temperature be?
   b) Why does Marie not heat up to this temperature?

110. An electric shower heating unit is rated at 240 V, 7 kW.
   a) Calculate the mass of water at 50 °C which this shower could deliver each second, if the input temperature is 15 °C.
   b) Solar heating panels were used to raise the input temperature of the water to 35 °C. What heater rating would be needed for the shower, in order to heat the same mass of water to the same final temperature?

SPACE

DISTANCES IN SPACE

1. How far is 1 light year in metres?

2. The Sun is 1.5×10^{11} m away from the Earth.
   How long does it take light to reach us from the Sun?

3. Light from Pluto takes 5.32 h to reach the Earth. How far away is Pluto?

4. Ursa Major is a collection of stars. Ursa Major is 1×10^7 light years away from the Earth.
   a) How far is this in kilometres?
   b) What name could be used to describe Ursa Major?

5. The Andromeda Galaxy is 1.9×10^{19} m away from the Earth.
   How far is this in light years?

6. Uranus is 2.7×10^{12} m away from the Earth.
   a) How long does it take light to reach the Earth from Uranus?
   b) What percentage of a light year is this distance?

7. The Moon is 3.84×10^8 m away from the Earth.
   a) How long does it take light to reach the Earth from the Moon?
   b) What percentage of a light year is this distance?
   c) The Apollo spacecraft took 100 h to reach the Moon.
      Calculate its average speed.

8. It takes 9 years for light from Sirius to reach us on the Earth.
   a) How far away is Sirius in metres?
   b) How long would it take to reach Sirius travelling at 1200 m s^{-1}?

9. The nearest star, apart from the Sun, is 4.07×10^{16} m away from the Earth.
   a) How long would it take to travel to the star at the speed of light?
   b) How long would it take to travel to the star at 1200 m s^{-1}?
   c) How long would it take to travel to the star at 30 m s^{-1} (70 m.p.h.)?

10. The nearest galaxy is 1.9×10^{19} m away.
    a) How long would it take to travel to the galaxy at the speed of light?
    b) How long would it take to travel to the galaxy at 1200 m s^{-1}?
    c) How long would it take to travel to the galaxy at 30 m s^{-1} (70 mph)?

11. If there are 10 thousand million galaxies in the Universe and each galaxy contains 100 thousand million stars, calculate the number of stars in the Universe.

Standard Grade Physics

TELESCOPES

12. **a)** Copy and complete the following diagram to show the passage of two rays of light from a very distant object through the telescope:

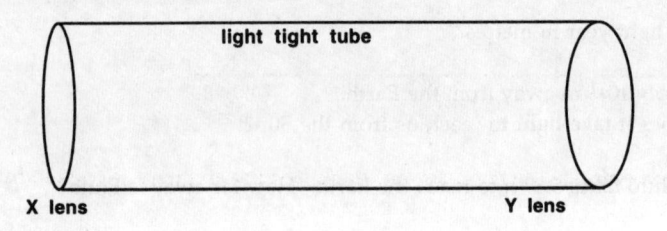

light tight tube

X lens   Y lens

b) Name the two lenses, X and Y.

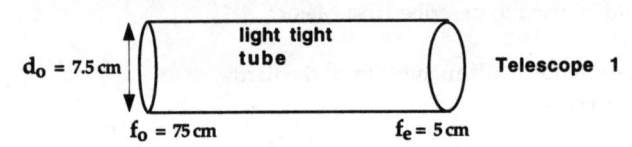

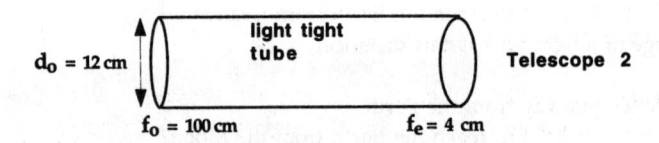

13.

Telescope 1: $d_o = 7.5$ cm, $f_o = 75$ cm, $f_e = 5$ cm

Telescope 2: $d_o = 12$ cm, $f_o = 100$ cm, $f_e = 4$ cm

a) Which telescope collects most light?
b) Which telescope gives the brightest picture?
c) If the objective lens has a focal length fo and the eyepiece lens a focal length fe, the total length of the tube is fo + fe.
   Which telescope is longer?
d) The overall magnification of the telescope is given by $\frac{f_o}{f_e}$.
   i) Calculate the magnification for telescope 1.
   ii) Calculate the magnification for telescope 2.

14. A telescope has an objective lens with a focal length of 80 cm and an eyepiece lens of focal length 4 cm.
    a) What is the total length of the tube?
    b) What is the overall magnification of the telescope?

15. A telescope has an objective lens with a focal length of 90 cm and an eyepiece lens of focal length 3.5 cm.
    a) What is the total length of the tube?
    b) What is the overall magnification of the telescope?

RAY DIAGRAMS

16. An object is placed in front of a convex lens as shown.

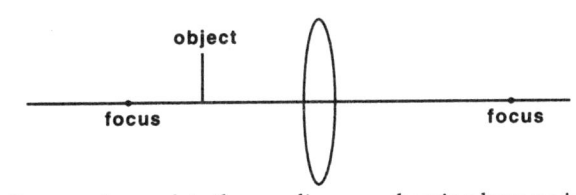

   ```
              object
                |
   ————————————|————(   )————————————
       focus       (   )    focus
                    (   )
   ```

   a) Copy and complete the ray diagram, showing how an image is formed by the lens.
   b) Describe the image formed - size; position; erect or inverted; real or virtual.

17. An object, 1 cm tall, is placed 3 cm in front of a convex lens with a focal length of 10 cm.
    a) Draw an accurate ray diagram to find the image produced.
    b) Describe the image formed - size; position; erect or inverted; real or virtual.

18. An object, 1 cm tall, is placed 6 cm in front of a convex lens with a focal length of 10 cm.
    a) Draw an accurate ray diagram to find the image produced.
    b) Describe the image formed - size; position; erect or inverted; real or virtual.

19. *An object, 1 cm tall, is placed in front of a convex lens with a focal length of 4 cm.*
    a) i) *Draw a ray diagram to scale showing the formation of the image when the object is placed 2 cm from the lens.*
       ii) *Describe the image formed.*
    b) i) *Draw a ray diagram to scale showing the formation of the image when the object is placed 8 cm from the lens.*
       ii) *Describe the image formed.*

20. *An object, 1 cm tall, is placed in front of a convex lens with a focal length of 5 cm.*
    a) i) *Draw a ray diagram to scale showing the formation of the image when the object is placed 4 cm from the lens.*
       ii) *Describe the image formed.*
    b) i) *Draw a ray diagram to scale showing the formation of the image when the object is placed 10 cm from the lens.*
       ii) *Describe the image formed.*

21. Consider your answers to Q.17 to Q.20.
    a) What can you say about the image formed when the object is placed at a distance which is twice the focal length away from the object.
    b) What can you say about the image formed as the object is moved closer to the focus, from a distance less than the focal length **or** a distance more than the focal length.

Standard Grade Physics

VISIBLE SPECTRUM

22. The visible spectrum has a range of wavelengths from approximately 400 nm to 700 nm in air.
    a) Calculate the minimum frequency that humans can see.
    b) Calculate the maximum frequency that humans can see.

23. Copy and complete the following diagrams:

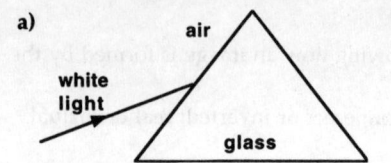

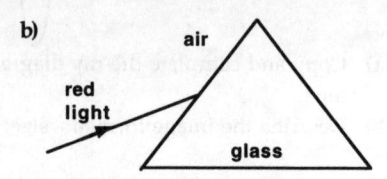

    a) white light → air / glass (prism)

    b) red light → air / glass (prism)

24. The information in the following table compares other stars to our Sun.

Star	Temperature	Diameter	Brightness	Colour
Sun	5800 °C	1.0	1	yellow
B Centauri	19 000 °C	6.0	4000	white
Altair	8200 °C	1.9	15	blue
Cygni A	3900 °C	0.7	0.1	red
Vega	10 600 °C	2.6	100	bluish-white
Betelgeuse	4750 °C	600	0.4	orange-red

    Another star has a temperature of 7000 °C.
    a) Suggest how bright the star may be.
    b) What colour is it likely to have?

25. List the colours of the visible spectrum in order of:
    a) increasing wavelength,
    b) increasing frequency.

26. The colour of a wave varies with the wavelength in nanometres as shown.

red	orange	yellow	green	blue	indigo	violet
700	650	600	550	500	450	400

    λ in nm

    a) What wavelength and colour of wave has a frequency of 6.25×10^{14} Hz?
    b) What wavelength and colour of wave has a frequency of 4.5×10^{14} Hz?
    c) What wavelength and colour of wave has a frequency of 5.1×10^{14} Hz?

ELECTROMAGNETIC SPECTRUM

27. a) List the radiations of the electromagnetic spectrum in order of:
    i) increasing frequency,
    ii) increasing wavelength.
    b) What do all radiations in the electromagnetic spectrum have in common?

28. An infra red wave has a wavelength of 2.7×10^{-5} m. This infrared radiation is used to detect people buried by an earthquake.
    a) Calculate the frequency of the infrared wave.
    b) A series of pulses is sent out with a frequency of 2500 Hz.
       Calculate the period of the pulses.
    c) The waves reflect back and are received after 8 ns.
       How deep is the person buried?

29. An ultra violet wave has a frequency of 1.1×10^{15} m.
    a) Calculate the wavelength of the ultraviolet wave.
    b) The Sun is 1.5×10^8 km from the Earth.
       How long does it take for the ultraviolet rays to reach the Earth?

Use the diagram, which shows the approximate wavelengths in metres for the various parts of the electromagnetic spectrum, to answer **Qs. 30 to 32**.

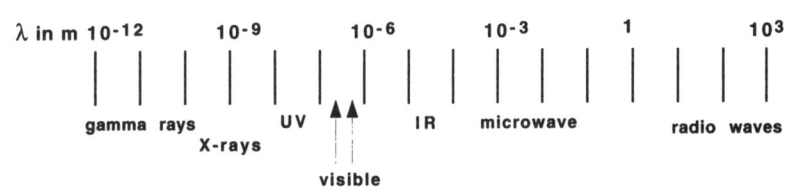

λ in m 10^{-12} 10^{-9} 10^{-6} 10^{-3} 1 10^3

gamma rays   UV   IR   microwave   radio waves
              X-rays
              visible

30. An electromagnetic wave has a frequency of 4.3×10^{12} Hz.
    a) Calculate the wavelength.
    b) State which part of the electromagnetic spectrum it belongs to.
    c) Suggest a suitable detector for the wave.
    d) How long would it take for a signal of this frequency to arrive from a comet 9×10^{13} m away?

31. An electromagnetic wave has a frequency of 5×10^{18} Hz.
    a) Calculate the wavelength.
    b) State which part of the electromagnetic spectrum it belongs to.
    c) Suggest a suitable detector for the wave.
    d) How far away is a star if a signal of this frequency takes 7×10^{18} s to arrive at Earth?

32. An electromagnetic wave has a frequency of 250 kHz.
    a) Calculate the wavelength.
    b) State which part of the electromagnetic spectrum it belongs to.
    c) Suggest a suitable detector for the wave.

Standard Grade Physics

NEWTON'S THIRD LAW

33. Draw a diagram showing the forces acting, and state all the 'Newton Pair' forces acting, in the following situations:
    a) a rocket at the instant it leaves the Earth
    b) an Olympic swimmer on the final length of a race
    c) two skaters pushing each other away on an ice rink

34. A man is playing golf. His club has a mass of 575 g and the ball has a mass of 45 g.
    a) The ball accelerates at 600 m s^{-2}. Calculate the force acting on the ball.
    b) The force acts for 2 x 10^{-2} s. Calculate the final speed of the ball.

35. A rugby ball has a mass of 400 g. The kicker gives it a momentary acceleration of 500 m s^{-2}.
    a) Calculate the force acting on the ball.
    b) What is the force acting on the kicker's foot?
    c) What is the direction of the force in part b)?

36. A rocket accelerates away from the Earth at 8 m s^{-2}. It has a mass of 1200 kg.
    a) Draw a diagram showing all the forces acting on the rocket.
    b) Calculate the weight of the rocket.
    c) Calculate the resultant force acting on the rocket.
    d) Calculate the force on the hot gases leaving the rocket?

37. Two skaters push each other away as part of a pair skating routine. The man has a mass of 70 kg while his partner has a mass of 45 kg. She accelerates away from him at 2.5 m s^{-2}.
    a) Calculate the force acting on her.
    b) State the force acting on him.
    c) Calculate his acceleration.

38. A girl steps out of a stationary rowing boat onto the shore. She has a mass of 65 kg and the boat has a mass of 25 kg. She pushes herself onto the shore with a force of 375 N.
    a) What is the force acting on the boat?
    b) What is the acceleration of the boat?
    c) If the force acts for 0.16 s, what is the final speed of the boat?
    d) How much kinetic energy does the boat gain?
    e) How much work is done by friction in stopping the boat?
    f) If the boat stops in a distance of 2.5 m, what is the average force due to friction with the water?

GRAVITATIONAL FIELD STRENGTH

39. The acceleration due to gravity on Earth is 10 m s^{-2}.
    a) What is the gravitational field strength on Earth in newtons per kilogram?
    b) What is the weight of a 45 kg boy on Earth?

40. The acceleration due to gravity on the Moon is 1.6 m s^{-2}.
    a) What is the gravitational field strength on the Moon in newtons per kilogram?
    b) What is the weight of a 65 kg astronaut on the Moon?

41. The gravitational field strength on Venus is 8.9 N kg^{-1}.
    a) What is the acceleration due to gravity on Venus?
    b) What would be the weight of a 2000 kg spacecraft on Venus?

42. The gravitational field strength on Mars is 3.7 N kg^{-1}.
    a) What is the acceleration due to gravity on Mars?
    b) What would be the weight of a 2000 kg spacecraft on Mars?

43. An astronaut has a mass of 550 N on Earth, where *g* = 10 N kg^{-1}.
    a) Calculate her mass on Earth.
    b) i) Calculate her mass on Mars, where *g* = 3.7 N kg^{-1}.
       ii) Calculate her weight on Mars.
    c) i) Calculate her mass on the Moon, where *g* = 1.6 N kg^{-1}.
       ii) Calculate her weight on the Moon.

44. A Lunar Rover was used to move around on the Moon's surface. It has a weight on Earth of 7000 N.
    a) Calculate the Rover's mass on Earth.
    b) i) Calculate the Rover's mass on the Moon, where *g* = 1.6 N kg^{-1}.
       ii) Calculate the Rover's weight on the Moon.
    c) i) Calculate the Rover's mass on Mars, where *g* = 3.7 N kg^{-1}.
       ii) Calculate the Rover's weight on Mars.

45. The gravitational field strength at 36 000 km above Earth is 0.22 N kg^{-1}.
    a) Calculate the weight of a satellite with a mass of 350 kg?
    b) *How long would the satellite take to orbit the Earth at this height?*
    c) What name is given to such a satellite?
    d) *What is particularly important about the orbit of such a satellite?*

46. The gravitational field strength at a height of 7000 km above Earth is 2.14 N kg^{-1}.
    a) What would be the weight of an astronaut of mass 65 kg, when in a spacecraft orbiting at this height?
    b) In fact the astronaut experiences weightlessness. Explain why this happens.

Standard Grade Physics

PROJECTILES

47. A ball is thrown vertically upwards. It leaves the hand at 25 m s^{-1}.
    a) How long does it take to reach the top of the flight where its final speed is zero?
    b) How long will it take to fall back down to the hand?
    c) What speed will it be travelling at when it reaches the hand?
    d) Sketch a speed - time graph for the ball's flight.
    e) Calculate the total distance travelled by the ball.

48. A ball is dropped out of a window. At the moment it is released the initial speed is zero. It takes 3 s to reach the ground.
    a) Calculate the final speed of the ball just before it touches the ground.
    b) Sketch a speed - time graph for the ball's flight.
    c) Calculate the total distance travelled by the ball.

49. A package is dropped from a helicopter which is hovering at rest. The package takes 8 s to reach the ground.
    a) Describe the forces acting on the helicopter as it hovers.
    b) Calculate the final speed of the package just before it touches the ground.
    c) Calculate the total distance travelled by the package.

50. A ball is thrown out of a window with a horizontal speed of 10 m s^{-1}. At the moment it is released out of the window the initial vertical speed is zero. It takes 4 s to reach the ground.
    a) What is the value of the horizontal acceleration of the ball?
    b) State the final horizontal speed of the ball just before it touches the ground.
    c) Sketch a speed - time graph for the ball's horizontal motion.
    d) Calculate the total horizontal distance travelled by the ball.
    e) What is the value of the vertical acceleration of the ball?
    f) Calculate the final vertical speed of the ball just before it touches the ground.
    g) Sketch a speed - time graph for the ball's vertical motion.
    h) Calculate the total vertical distance travelled by the ball.

51. A cat jumps horizontally out of a window with a speed of 5 m s^{-1}. It takes 1.5 s to reach the ground.
    a) State the final horizontal speed of the cat.
    b) Calculate the final vertical speed of the cat.
    c) Sketch a speed - time graph for the cat's horizontal motion.
    d) Calculate the total horizontal distance travelled by the cat.
    e) Sketch a speed - time graph for the cat's vertical motion.
    f) Calculate the total vertical distance travelled by the cat.

52. A plane is flying horizontally at 180 m s⁻¹ when it drops a bomb. The bomb hits the ground 9 s later.
    a) State the final horizontal speed of the bomb just before it touches the ground.
    b) Calculate the final vertical speed of the bomb just before it touches the ground.
    c) Calculate the total horizontal distance travelled by the bomb.
    d) Sketch a speed - time graph for the bomb's vertical motion.
    e) Calculate the total vertical distance travelled by the bomb.
    f) Where is the plane, compared to the bomb, at the moment that the bomb hits the ground, provided it does not alter course?

53. A plane is flying horizontally at 400 m s⁻¹ when it drops a bomb. The bomb hits the ground 20 s later.
    a) State the final horizontal speed of the bomb just before it touches the ground.
    b) Calculate the final vertical speed of the bomb just before it touches the ground.
    c) Calculate the total horizontal distance travelled by the bomb.
    d) Sketch a speed - time graph for the bomb's vertical motion.
    e) Calculate the total vertical distance travelled by the bomb.
    f) Where is the plane, compared to the bomb, at the moment that the bomb hits the ground, provided it does not alter course?

54. A ball rolls across a table at 5 m s⁻¹ then reaches the edge and rolls off. The ball lands 2.5 m from the table.
    a) State the final horizontal speed of the ball just before it touches the ground.
    b) Calculate the time it takes for the ball to land.
    c) What is the inital vertical speed of the ball?
    d) What is the vertical acceleration of the ball?
    e) Calculate the final vertical speed of the ball just before it touches the ground.
    f) Sketch a speed - time graph for the ball's vertical motion.
    g) Calculate the total vertical distance travelled by the ball.

55. A package leaves a helicopter with a horizontal speed of 25 m s⁻¹. The package lands 125 m in front of the point where it left the helicopter.
    a) Calculate the time it takes for the package to land.
    b) What is the inital vertical speed?
    c) What is the vertical acceleration?
    d) Calculate the final vertical speed of the package just before it touches the ground.
    e) Sketch a speed - time graph for the package's vertical motion.
    f) Calculate the height of the helicopter.

ROCKETS AND SPACE CRAFT

56. A rocket has a mass of 1850 kg and the engine can produce a thrust of 30 kN.
    a) Calculate the weight of the rocket.
    b) Draw a diagram showing all the forces acting on the rocket at take off.
    c) Calculate the initial acceleration of the rocket.

57. A rocket has a mass of 10^4 kg and the engine can produce a thrust of 200 kN.
    a) Calculate the weight of the rocket.
    b) Draw a diagram showing all the forces acting on the rocket at take off.
    c) What is the initial acceleration of the rocket?
    d) The rocket burns up 3000 kg of fuel in the 10 s after take off.
       Calculate the new weight of the rocket, assuming *g* to be unchanged.
    e) What is the acceleration now, assuming the thrust remains constant?

58. The diagram shows a cut-away of a rocket.

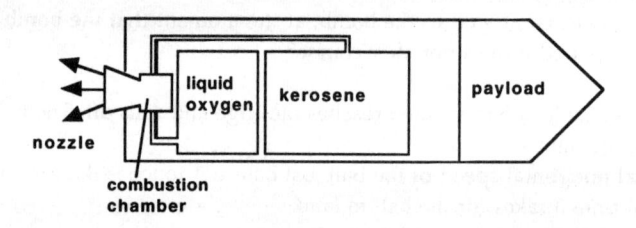

    a) There are 3×10^5 tonnes of kerosene (1 tonne = 1000 kg) and it is burnt at the rate of 4.5×10^3 kg s^{-1}. How long does it take to run out of kerosene?
    b) The payload then separates from the rest of the rocket. The payload has a mass of 950 kg and is travelling at a speed of 3080 m s^{-1}.
       Calculate the kinetic energy of the payload.

59. The space shuttle uses two solid rocket boosters. Each booster rocket contains 560 tonnes of fuel (1 tonne = 1000 kg). Each rocket burns 4700 kg every second.
    a) For how long does the fuel last?
    b) The booster rockets are jettisoned and return to Earth when the shuttle is travelling at 1200 m s^{-1}. Calculate the kinetic energy of one of the rockets if it has a mass of 9×10^4 kg.
    c) The rocket tank is made of several materials but heats up as though it had an average specific heat capacity of 650 J kg^{-1} $°C^{-1}$. It does not melt. Calculate the rise in temperature produced if all the kinetic energy becomes heat energy

60. A meteor enters the Earth's atmosphere at 30 000 m s⁻¹. It has a mass of 880 g and is made of material with an average specific heat capacity of 570 J kg⁻¹ °C⁻¹. The material melts between 1500 °C and 2200 °C.
   a) Calculate the kinetic energy of the meteor.
   b) What happens to the speed of the meteor as it hits the atmosphere? Explain.
   c) If all the kinetic energy becomes heat energy and is used to change the temperature of the meteor, calculate the maximum change in temperature of the meteor, if it remained solid.
   d) Why does the meteor not reach the Earth?

61. A meteorite hits the Earth's atmosphere at 28 000 m s⁻¹. It has a mass of 1400 g and is made of material with an average specific heat capacity of 570 J kg⁻¹ °C⁻¹. The material melts between 1500 °C and 2200 °C.
   a) Calculate the kinetic energy of the meteorite.
   b) If all the kinetic energy becomes heat energy and is used to change the temperature of the meteorite, calculate the maximum change in temperature of the meteorite (assume it remains solid).
   c) What will have happened to the mass of the solid meteorite before it reaches the surface of the Earth?

62. A space capsule with a mass of 1440 kg re-enters the Earth's atmosphere at 24 000 m s⁻¹. The capsule has an average specific heat capacity of 970 J kg⁻¹ °C⁻¹.
   a) Calculate the kinetic energy of the capsule on re-entry.
   b) If all the kinetic energy were to become heat energy of the caspsule, calculate the predicted final temperature of the capsule assuming no change of state.
   c) Suggest how the capsule is designed to radiate heat away and to protect the men inside the capsule.

63. A satellite has a mass of 480 kg and is travelling at a speed of 4500 m s⁻¹. It needs to slow down to 3750 m s⁻¹ in the same direction, in order to move into the correct orbit.
   a) Calculate the original kinetic energy of the satellite.
   b) Calculate the final kinetic energy of the satellite.
   c) A, B, C and D are small thruster rockets positioned as shown on the diagram.

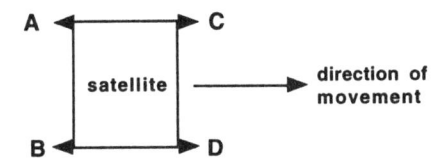

   How can they be used to slow down the satellite?

Standard Grade Physics

64. The Lunar Rover, mass 750 kg, had a top speed of 5 km h^{-1}
   a) What was the speed of the Lunar Rover in metres per second.
   b) Calculate the maximum kinetic energy of the Lunar Rover.
   c) The engine was turned off and the vehicle coasted to a stop from its top speed over 25 m. What was the average force due to friction?

65. A satellite has solar cells to provide electrical power. The Sun can provide 1375 W m^{-2} of power.
   a) The satellite has 4 m^2 of solar cells.
      How much power would these provide if the solar cells were 100% efficient?
   b) In fact the cells are only 20% efficient.
      How much power is actually provided?
   c) If the electrical system of the satellite has to work at 12 V, what would be the total current available?

66. A spacecraft has solar cells to provide electrical power. The Sun can provide 750 W m^{-2} of power.
   a) The spacecraft has 9 m^2 of solar cells. How much power would these provide if the solar cells were 100% efficient?
   b) In fact the cells are only 23% efficient.
      How much power is actually provided?
   c) If the electrical system of the space craft has to work at 12 V, what would be the total current available?

67. A spacecraft of mass 875 kg slows down from 10 000 m s^{-1} to 500 m s^{-1} as it comes down through the Earth's atmosphere.
   a) Calculate the original kinetic energy of the spacecraft.
   b) Calculate the final kinetic energy of the spacecraft.
   c) If the spacecraft travels 1.5 x 10^5 km through the atmosphere as it comes into land, what is the average force due to friction?

GRAPHS

1. A graph of force, **F**, against acceleration, **a**, is shown below.

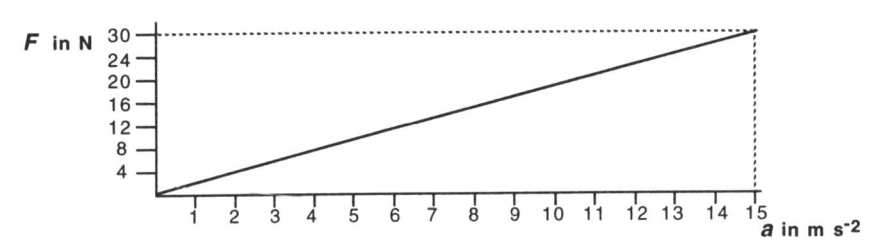

   F in N, axis values: 4, 8, 12, 16, 20, 24, 30
   a in m s^{-2}, axis values: 1–15

   a) From the graph, what is the relationship between force and acceleration?
   b) From the gradient of the slope, calculate the mass of the object.

2. A graph of distance, **d**, against time, **t**, is shown below.

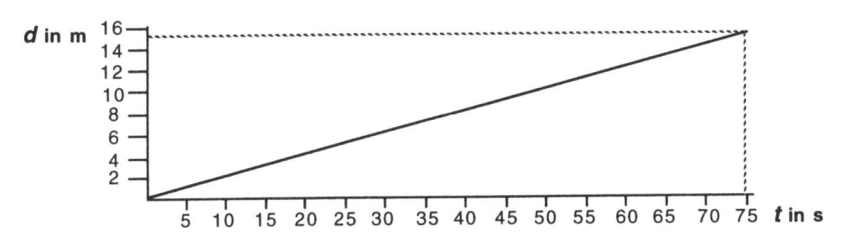

   d in m, axis values: 2, 4, 6, 8, 10, 12, 14, 16
   t in s, axis values: 5–75

   a) From the graph, what is the relationship between distance and time?
   b) From the gradient of the slope, calculate the speed of the object.

3. A graph of energy, **E**, against time, **t**, is shown below.

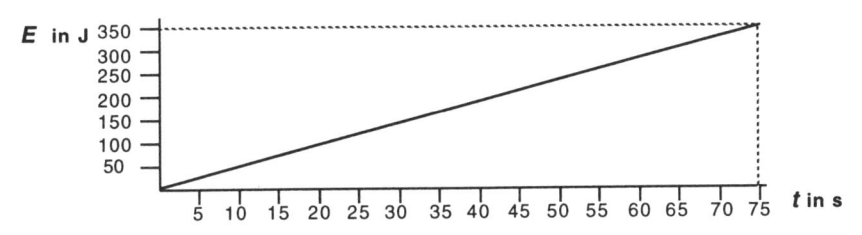

   E in J, axis values: 50, 100, 150, 200, 250, 300, 350
   t in s, axis values: 5–75

   a) From the graph, what is the relationship between energy and time?
   b) From the gradient of the slope, calculate the power of the object.

Standard Grade Physics

4. A graph of voltage, **V**, against current, **I**, is shown below.

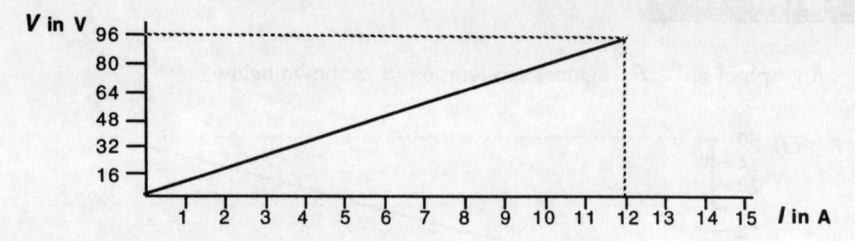

   a) From the graph, what is the relationship between voltage and current?
   b) From the gradient of the slope, calculate the resistance of the resistor.

5. A graph of power, **P**, against voltage, **V**, for a resistor is shown below.

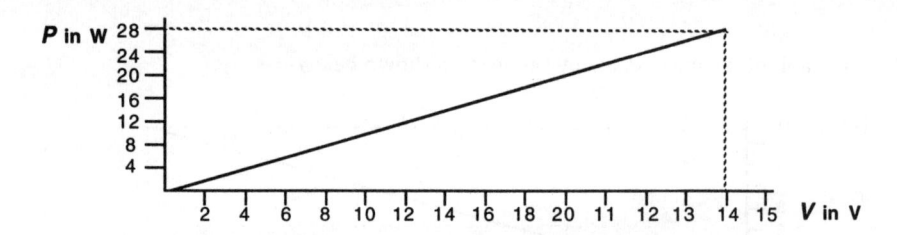

   a) From the graph, what is the relationship between power and voltage?
   b) From the gradient of the slope, calculate the current through the resistor.

6. A graph of work done, E_W, against distance, **d**, is shown below.

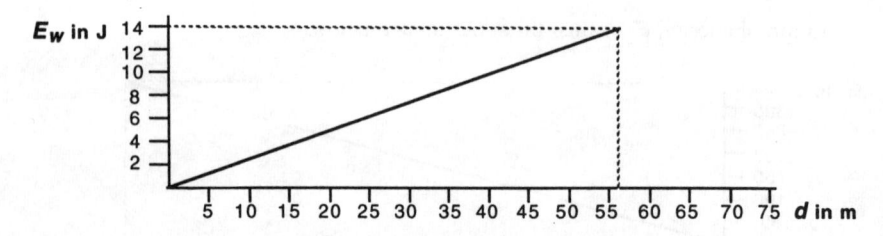

   a) From the graph, what is the relationship between E_W and **d**?
   b) From the gradient of the slope, calculate the force on the object.

7. A graph of charge, **Q**, against time, **t**, is shown below.

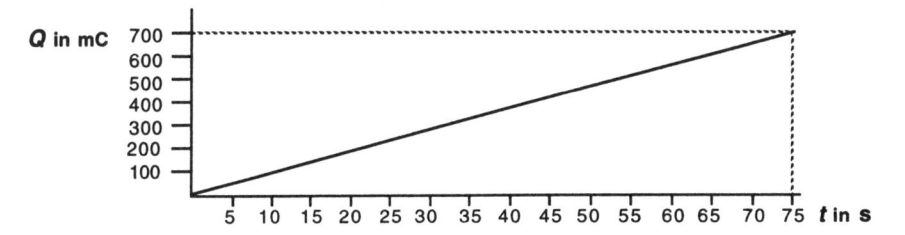

Q in mC, *t* in s

a) From the graph, what is the relationship between charge and time?
b) From the gradient of the slope, calculate the capacitance of the capacitor.

8. A graph of pressure, **P**, against, **1/V**, is shown below.

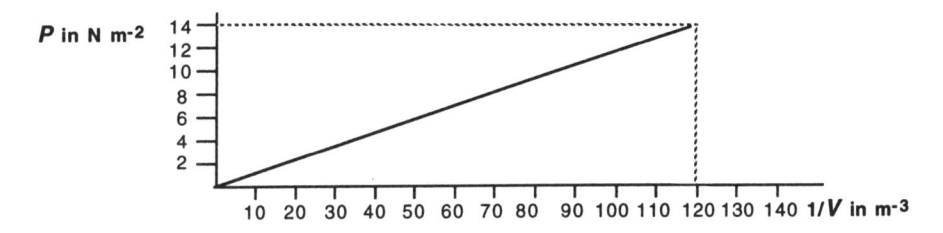

P in N m^{-2}, 1/*V* in m^{-3}

a) From the graph, what is the relationship between *P* and 1/*V*?
b) What can you say about pressure x volume?

Standard Grade Physics 111

FORMULAE

Formulae are given in the topic heading where they occur first. They may be required in other topics.

$c = 3 \times 10^8$ m s^{-1}

TELECOMMUNICATIONS

$d = v t$ (for constant speed)

$v = f \lambda$

$f = \dfrac{1}{T}$

USING ELECTRICITY

$Q = I t$

$V = I R$

$E = P t$

$P = I V$ $P = I^2 R$ $P = \dfrac{V^2}{R}$

$P = I V$ $P = I^2 R$ $P = \dfrac{V^2}{R}$

$E = P t$ $E = I V t = I^2 R \times t = \dfrac{V^2}{R} \times t$

$R_S = R_1 + R_2 + \ldots\ldots$ resistors in series

$\dfrac{1}{R_P} = \dfrac{1}{R_1} + \dfrac{1}{R_2} + \ldots\ldots$ resistors in parallel

HEALTH PHYSICS

power of lens $= \dfrac{1}{\text{focal length (in metres)}}$

ELECTRONICS

$V_{R_1} = \dfrac{R_1}{R_{total}} \times V_{supply}$ **VOLTAGE DIVIDERS**

voltage gain $= \dfrac{\text{output voltage}}{\text{input voltage}}$

power gain $= \dfrac{\text{output power}}{\text{input power}}$

TRANSPORT

$a = \dfrac{v - u}{t}$ $v = u + at$

$W = mg$

$F = ma$

$E_w = Fd$

$E_p = mgh$

$E_k = \tfrac{1}{2}mv^2$

$E_p = E_k \Rightarrow v = \sqrt{(2gh)}$ (Do not use if energy is 'lost' due to friction.)

Distance = area under speed - time graph

$\overline{v}$ = average speed = $\dfrac{\text{total distance gone}}{\text{total time taken}}$

ENERGY

%Efficiency = $\dfrac{E_{out}}{E_{in}} \times 100\%$ = $\dfrac{P_{out}}{P_{in}} \times 100\%$

$\dfrac{V_s}{V_p} = \dfrac{N_s}{N_p} = \dfrac{I_p}{I_s}$

$E_h = cm\Delta T$ with NO change of state

$E_h = mL$ with a change of state

   $L_{vaporisation}$ - if boiling or condensing

   L_{fusion} - if melting or freezing

Standard Grade Physics

Abbreviations | Units

d	distance	metre	m
v	velocity	metres per second	m s⁻¹
t	time	second	s
f	frequency	Hertz	Hz
λ	wavelength	metre	m
T	period	second	s
Q	charge	coulomb	C
I	current	amp	A
V	voltage	volt	V
R	resistance	ohm	Ω
E	energy	joule	J
P	power	watt	W
W	weight	gram	g
m	mass	kilkogram	Kg
g	gravitational force	newtons per kilogram	N kg⁻¹
F	force	newton	N
a	acceleration	metres per square second	m s⁻²
E_w	work done	joule	J
h	height	metre	m
E_k	kinetic energy	joule	J
E_p	potential energy	joule	J
V_s	voltage at secondary		
V_p	voltage at primary		
N_s	number of turns at secondary		
N_p	number of turns at primary		
I_p	current at primary		
I_s	current at secondary		
Δ*T*	change in temperature		°C
L	latent heat		J Kg⁻¹
C	specific heat capacity		J Kg⁻¹ °C⁻¹
	power of lens	dioptre	D

ANSWERS

BASIC MATHEMATICS

1. a) 3.7×10^8 b) 2.005×10^{10}
   c) 9.3×10^{14} d) 2.3×10^{-4}
   e) 6×10^{-8} f) 4×10^{-11}

2. a) 300 000 000   b) 27 500
   c) 7 004 000 000   d) 0.0084
   e) 0.000 000 042   f) 0.000 090 8

3. a) 5000 V   b) 0.023 V
   c) 0.000 007 V   d) 2 800 000 V
   e) 0.000 000 067 V   f) 0.000 389 V

4. a) 8 MJ   b) 4 µJ
   c) 6.34 kJ   d) 5 mJ
   e) 63 µJ   f) 9.806 MJ

5. a) 50 000 m   b) 30 000 000 m
   c) 0.057 m   d) 0.09 m
   e) 8310 m   f) 25 356.28

6. a) 300 s   b) 10 800 s
   c) 160 s   d) 502 s
   e) 447 s   f) 26 730 s

7. a) 0.5 kg   b) 7400 kg
   c) 0.000 25 kg   d) 0.0975 kg
   e) 4.5×10^{-8} kg   f) 3.7×10^6 kg

8. a) 0.8 A   b) 250 000 A
   c) 375 000 A   d) 0.000 035 6 A
   e) 35 600 A   f) 9.43 A

9. a) 0.75 V   b) 4 700 000 V
   c) 450 000 V   d) 0.000 053 V
   e) 281 000 V   f) 10.67 V

10. a) 56 000 J   b) 0.078 J
    c) 8 000 000 000 J   d) 0.000 000 3 J
    e) 7500 J   f) 0.0036 J

11. a) 54.3   b) 1240
    c) 29.7   d) 3 260 000
    e) 0.855   f) 2 570 000

TELECOMMUNICATIONS

1. a) 100 m   b) 6 m s^{-1}
   c) 8 s   d) 4 m s^{-1}
   e) 140 s   f) 112.5 m
   g) 12 m s^{-1}
2. 1700 m
3. 332.5 m s^{-1}
4. 9 s
5. a) 2720 m
   b) light arrives instantaneously
6. 1500 m s^{-1}
7. 337.5 km
8. 0.79 s
9. 3500 m s^{-1}
10. a) 3×10^9 m
    b) 9×10^{10} m
11. a) 1320 -> 1360 m
    b) 4.4 -> 4.5×10^{-6} s
12. 1.5×10^{-3} s
13. 0.67 s
14. a) 0.76 s   b) 0.05 s
    c) Carol
15. a) 81.6 m   b) 40.8 m
16. a) 1725 m   b) 637.5 m
17. 42.5 m
18. 255 m
19. a) 12.5 cm   b) 2 m
20. a) 5 Hz   b) 0.2 s
21. a) 4 Hz   b) 20 cm
    c) 0.25 s   d) 0.6 m
    e) i) **A** - crest
       ii) **B** - trough
    f) i) 70 cm   ii) 10 cm
22. a) 12.5 m   b) 0.4 Hz
    c) 2.5 s   d) 5 m s^{-1}
23. a) 8 Hz   b) 0.125 s

Standard Grade Physics

24. a) 0.167 Hz b) 15 m
    c) 2.5 m s⁻¹
25. a) i) 0.125 s ii) 56 m s⁻¹
    b) i) 4 Hz ii) 9 m
    c) i) 1200 Hz ii) 8.3 × 10⁻⁴ s
    d) i) 16 000 Hz ii) 0.02 m
    e) i) 5 × 10⁻⁸ s ii) 3 × 10⁸ m s⁻¹
    f) i) 80 Hz ii) 0.0125 s
    g) i) 2.3 × 10⁻⁶ m ii) 2.67 × 10⁻⁴ s
26. 25.5 m s⁻¹
27. 3333 Hz
28. a) 2 m b) 0.11 s
29. 6 × 10¹⁴ Hz
30. 0.024 m
31. 1.05 × 10⁶ Hz
32. 102 m
33. a) 1.6 Hz b) 3 m
34. 1.2 × 10⁻³ m
35. a) 72 m s⁻¹ b) 4320 m
36. a) 8 Hz; 0.125 s b) 0.4 m s⁻¹
    c) 120 s
37. a) 2.7 m s⁻¹ b) 810 m
38. a) 2 m s⁻¹ b) 40 Hz
    c) 0.025 s
39. a) 1500 m s⁻¹ b) 1333 Hz
    c) 1.125 m
40. a) 66.7 m s⁻¹ b) 267 Hz
    c) 3.75 × 10⁻³ s
41. 4 s
42. 8400 m
43. a) 1.5 m s⁻¹ b) 292.5 m
44. a) 1.03 mm b) 1.79 × 10¹⁴ Hz
    c) 2.46 mm
45. $d = \lambda$ when $t = T$
    $d = v\,t \Rightarrow \lambda = v\,T$ but $T = \frac{1}{f}$
    $\lambda = \frac{v}{f} \Rightarrow v = f\lambda$
46. i) tuner ii) decoder
    iii) amplifier iv) battery
47. a) loudspeaker b) tuner
    c) decoder d) power supply
    e) amplifier f) aerial
48. a) changing the carrier signal by adding the audio signal
    b) i)
    ii)
49. 1.8 × 10¹⁰ m
50. 2.2 × 10⁻³ s
51. a)

station	frequency
Radio 2	88 MHz
Radio 3	90 MHz
Radio Scotland	93 MHz
Radio 4	95 MHz
Radio 1	98 MHz

   b) 3.23 m
   c) the tuner
   d) 101 MHz
52. Electrons hit screen, lose kinetic energy and light energy is produced. The beam sweeps across the screen 625 times to form one picture. 25 pictures are formed every second, each slightly different. Humans only see changes 20 times a second. The image remains on the retina and is seen as moving pictures.
53. red, green, blue
54. a) magenta b) cyan
    c) yellow d) pink
    e) pale blue f) white
55. aerial → tuner → vision decoder → vision amplifier → TV tube; tuner → audio decoder → sound amplifier → loudspeaker
56. a) 1500 b) 9.375 × 10⁵
    c) 7500
57. a) 0.04 s b) 6.4 × 10⁻⁵ s
    c) 7031 m s⁻¹
58. a) 0.482 m to 0.475 m
    b) to send information for picture and sound

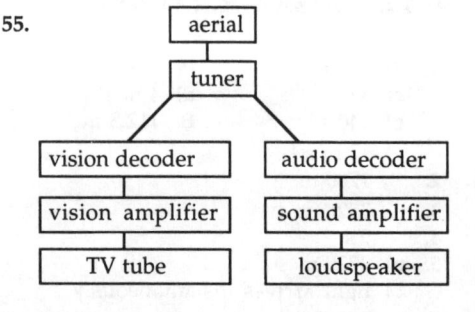

59. a) 800 MHz to 809 MHz
    b) 4×10^{-4} s
60. a) so signals do not become mixed up.
    b) 1.67 m
    c) i) an aerial
       ii) metal of car reflects radio waves away if no aerial
    d) Both have limited power and thus limited geographical ranges which do not overlap.
61. a) diffraction
    b) long wavelength
62. a) 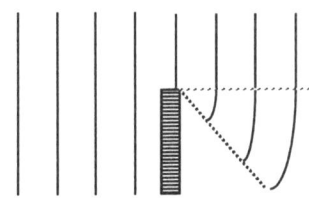
    b) 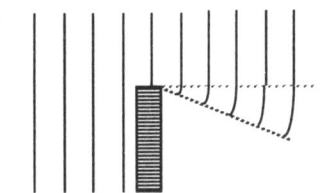
    c) 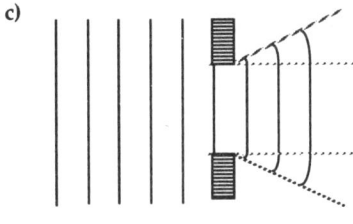
    d) 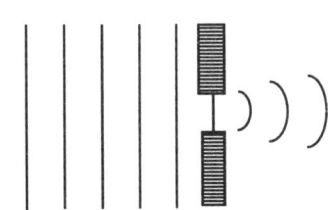
63. reflection
64. a) 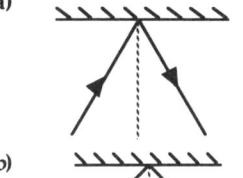
    b) 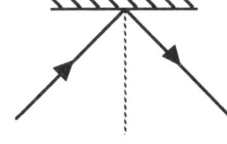
    c) 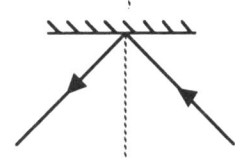
    d) 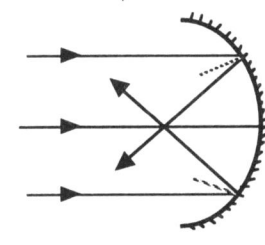
    e) 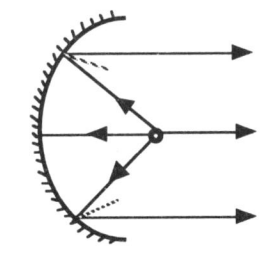
65. Light travelling from more dense material to less dense, meets boundary at angle greater than the critical angle and is all reflected.
66. a)
    b)
    c) total internal reflection
    d) critical angle

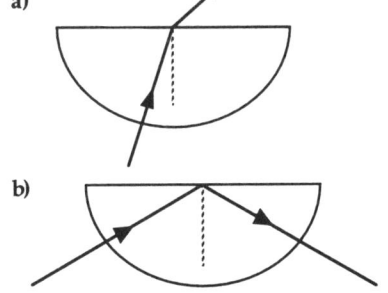

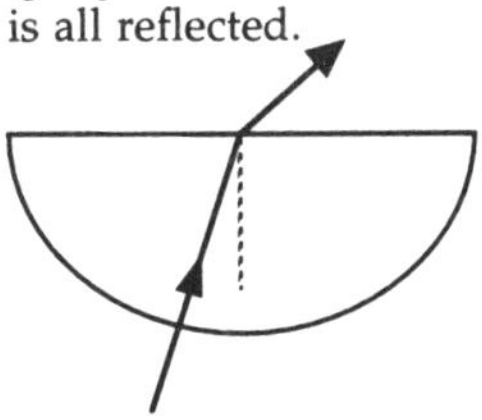

Standard Grade Physics   117

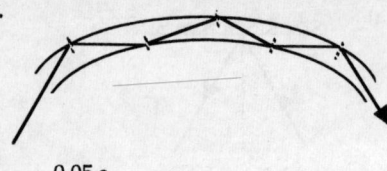

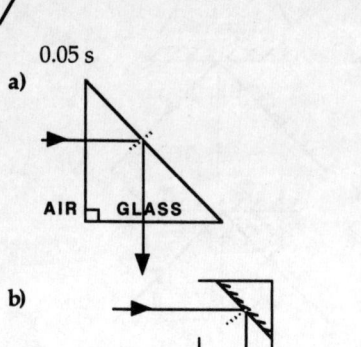

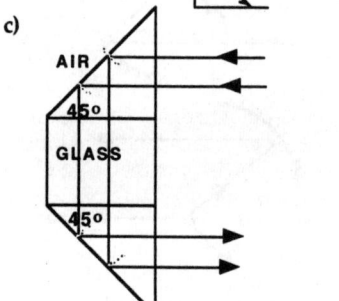

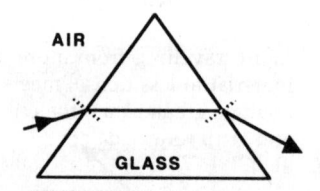

67. [diagram of wave reflecting off curved surface]

68. 0.05 s

69. a) [diagram: ray entering glass from air through right-angle prism]

   b) [diagram: ray reflecting through two angled mirrors]

   c) [diagram: 45° glass prism with AIR, showing rays]

   d) [diagram: triangular prism with AIR outside, GLASS inside, ray refracting through]

70. the height above the Earth's surface

71. a) one which stays above the same point on the Earth's surface
    b) 24 hours
    c) above the equator
    d) three
    e) 36 000 km

72. a) less than 24 hours (2 to 8 h)
    b) 24 h
    c) more than 24 hours (about 36 h)

73. a) provides parallel beam
    b) collects energy over large area and focuses on aerial

74. a) so incoming and outgoing waves do not get mixed up
    b) 57.7 mm; 53.6 mm
    c) signal is amplified

75. a) 90 min
    b) The pictures could only be seen from Britain for 20 min out of 90.
    c) 0.27 s
    d) 2×10^9 Hz

76. a) 18   b) 30
    c) 5   d) 3216

USING ELECTRICITY

1. a) 5 A b) 60 C
   c) 180 s d) 1.35 C
   e) 4 A f) 2×10^5 s
   g) 7.5 A
2. 2 types
3. a) Charges repel.
   b) Charges repel.
   c) Charges attract.
4. 18 000 A
5. 0.18 C
6. 50 000 s
7. 5 A
8. 1.08 C
9. a) 840 C b) 22.5 C
   c) 1.4×10^{20}
10. a) cell
    b)  —|⊢--|⊢—
    c) resistor
    d) bulb
    e) (fuse symbol)
    f) capacitor
    g) 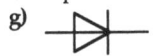 (diode symbol)
    h)  (variable resistor symbol)
11. a) 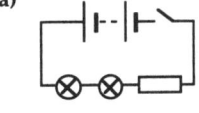 (circuit diagram)
    b) 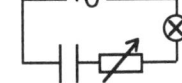 (circuit diagram)
12. a) 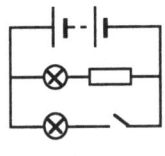 (circuit diagram)
    b) 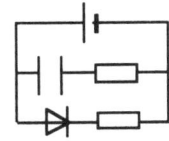 (circuit diagram)
13. a) 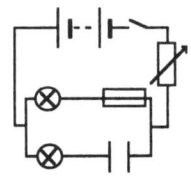 (circuit diagram)
    b) 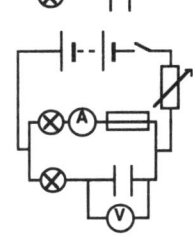 (circuit diagram)
14. a) The negative terminal of a cell is connected to a switch. The switch is in series with an ammeter, then a variable resistor and a bulb. The bulb is connected to the positive terminal.
    b) The negative terminal of a cell is connected to a diode in series with a switch, which is connected to the positive terminal. A resistor in series with a capacitor are in parallel with the diode and switch.
15. a) series b) parallel
    c) parallel d) series
16. a) 1, 2, 3, 4 b) 1, 3
    c) 2, 4 d) 1, 3, 4, 5
    e) 1
17. a) 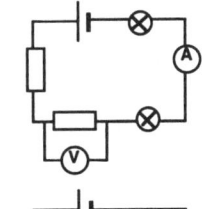 (circuit diagram)
    b) (circuit diagram)
    c) (circuit diagram)

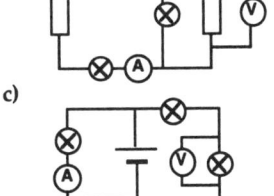

Standard Grade Physics

d) [circuit diagram]
   e) a.c. meters
18. a) switch open 1, 2, 3, 4, 5
       switch closed 4, 5
    b) switch open 1, 2, 3, 5
       switch closed 1, 5
19. [circuit diagram]
20. [circuit diagram]
21. [circuit diagram with boiler and fan]

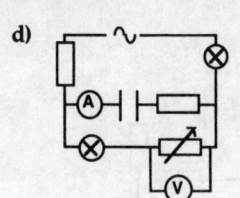

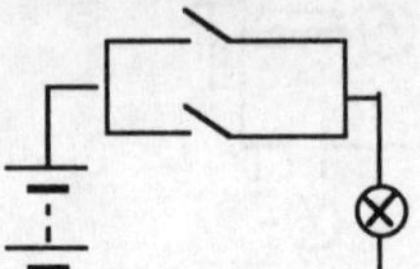

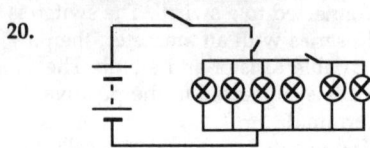

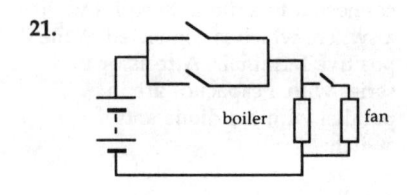

22. a) 8 Ω   b) 82.5 V
    c) 50 A   d) 21 000 V
    e) 3×10^7 Ω   f) 20 A
    g) 8×10^6 Ω
23. 42.9 mA
24. 360 kV
25. 800 000 Ω
26. a) 23 A   b) 23 mA
27. 180 Ω to 90 000 Ω
28. a) 2.73 A, 0.75 A, 0.33 A
    b) 3.81 A
29. a) 1.25 V, 1.5 V, 2.25 V
    b) 5 V
30. a) 500 J   b) 66.7 W
    c) 200 s   d) 2.3 mW
    e) 3.6×10^5 J f) 2×10^7 s
    g) 383 W
31. 1.3 W
32. 1.08×10^7 J
33. 92.6 h
34. 694 hours
35. 60 W
36. 1.06×10^8 J
37. those used for heating
38. a) 600 W   b) 100 W
    c) 3 kW   d) 3 kW
    e) 12 kW   f) 1 kW
39. a) 6 V   b) 12 A
    c) 6.25 mW   d) 0.5 A
    e) 30 V   f) 16 W
    g) 28.8 A
40. a) 0.02 W   b) 57.5 W
    c) 2875 W   d) 632.5 W
41. a) 8.7 A   b) 6.94 A
    c) 0.5 A   d) 4×10^{-5} A
42. a) 50 000 V   b) 4 V
    c) 120 V   d) 240 V
43. a) 200 V   b) 400 W
44. a) 8 mA   b) 3200 W
45. $P = IV$ but $V = IR$
    $= I.IR = I^2R$
46. a) 2 A   b) 1.8 W
    c) 4 Ω   d) 25.6 W
    e) 2.4 A   f) 2.4×10^8 Ω
    g) 49 W
47. a) 2.5 W   b) 31.25 W
    c) 0.612 W   d) 0.284 W
48. a) 200 000 Ω   b) 50 000 Ω
    c) 160 000 Ω   d) 125 Ω
49. a) 3 A   b) 0.8 A
    c) 6.32 A   d) 0.49 A
50. a) 2 A   b) 6.25 Ω
51. a) 4 mA   b) 48 mW
52. a) 20 V   b) 125 W
    c) 1000 Ω   d) 1 mW
    e) 40 kV   f) 800 V
    g) 0.36 W
53. a) 26.5 W   b) 13.3 mW
    c) 0.13 W   d) 0.09 W
54. a) 10.6 Ω   b) 6 Ω
    c) 2.57 Ω   d) 750 Ω
55. a) 12.2 V   b) 47.4 V
    c) 1.12 V   d) 118 kV
56. a) 5 Ω   b) 4 A
57. 230 V, 8.7 A
58. $P = IV$ but $I = \dfrac{V}{R}$
    $= \dfrac{V}{R} \cdot V = \dfrac{V^2}{R}$

59. a) i) 100 V ii) 10 A iii) 10 000 J
    b) i) 0.0125 A ii) 0.625 W iii) 6.25 J
    c) i) 25 W ii) 5000 V iii) 1 X 10^6 Ω
    d) i) 0.02 A ii) 1 mW iii) 10 mJ
    e) i) 240 V ii) 57.6 W iii) 576 J
    f) i) 1333 V ii) 44.4 Ω iii) 400 kJ
    g) i) 1200 W ii) 12 A iii) 8.3 Ω
60. a) 84 mA; 42 mA; 8.4 mA
    b) 3.53 W; 1.76 W; 0.353 W
    c) 5.64 W d) 1693 J
61. a) 2.8 V; 5.6 V; 28 V
    b) 36.4 V
    c) 15.7 mW; 31.4 mW; 157 mW
    d) 0.204 W e) 61.2 J
62. a) 27.8 W b) 5.18 Ω
    c) 2.3 A d) 12 500 C
63. 12.2 A, 245 V
64. a) 11.5 V b) 0.144 A
    c) 1.65 W d) 119 kJ
65. a) 50 Ω b) 0.1 A
    c) 7 V d) 70 Ω
66. a) 2400 J
    b) light and heat
    c) more efficient
67. a) 1.5 MW b) 1067 Ω
    c) 37.5 A
68. a) 2880 W b) 240 V
    c) 1042 s
69. a) 3000 W b) 17.6 Ω
    c) 13.04 A
70. a) 1.92 Ω b) 15 750 J
    c) kinetic, light d) 1312.5 C
71. 15 C
72. a) current constant
    b) voltages add up to supply
73. a) currents in branches add up to total current
    b) voltage same for all branches
74. a) 1.25 V; 6.25 V; 2.5 V
    b) 10 V c) 2.5 W
75. a) 2.4 A; 1.2 A; 0.48 A
    b) 4.08 A c) 48.96 W
76. a) 2 A; 2 A b) 4 A; 4 A; 4 A
    c) 1 A; 1 A; 1 A d) all at 3 A
    e) 1.2 A; 1.2 A; 1.8 A; 1.8 A
77. a) 6 V; 6 V b) 8 V; 8 V; 8 V
    c) all at 3 V
    d) 2 V; 2 V; 3 V; 3 V
    e) 6 V; 6 V; 4 V; 4 V; 4 V
78. a) 20 Ω; 5 Ω b) 6 Ω; 2 Ω
    c) 100 Ω; 200 Ω d) 30 Ω; 10 Ω

e) 6250 Ω; 1000 Ω f) 80 Ω; 26.7 Ω
g) 6 Ω; 18 Ω
79. a) 33 Ω b) 3 Ω
    c) 12 Ω d) 13.5 Ω
80. a) total resistance larger than largest resistor
    b) total resistance smaller than smallest resistor
81. 19.7 Ω
82. a) 44 Ω b) 33 Ω
    c) 18 Ω d) 16 Ω
83. a) 2 Ω b) 2.2 Ω
    c) 7.5 Ω d) 6.7 Ω
84. a) 5 Ω b) 12 Ω
    c) 25 Ω d) 0 Ω
85. 8.5 Ω
86. 7.3 Ω
87. 54 Ω
88. a) 24 Ω b) 0.5 A
    c) 3.5 V; 2.5 V; 6V
    d) 1.75 W; 1.25 W; 3W
89. a) 40 Ω b) 0.25 A
    c) 0.75 V; 2.5 V; 5 V; 1.75 V
    d) 0.188 W; 0.625 W; 1.25 W; 0.438 W
90. a) 4 Ω b) 18 V
    c) 3 A; 1.5 A d) 54 W; 27 W
91. a) 2.73 Ω b) 20 V
    c) 2 A; 4A; 1.3 A
    d) 40W; 80 W; 26.7 W
92. a) 6 Ω b) 2 A
    c) 8 V d) 4 V
    e) 0.67 A; 1.33 A,
    f) 32 W; 2.68 W; 5.32 W
93. a) 30 Ω b) 0.4 A
    c) 8 V d) 4 V,
    e) 0.13 A; 0.267 A
    f) 3.2 W; 0.65 W; 1.07 W
94. a) 3 Ω - 0.5 A; 1.5 V; 1.25 W
       12 Ω - 0.5 A; 6 V;   3 W
       4 Ω   - 0.375 A; 1.5 V; 0.563 W
       12 Ω - 0.125 A; 1.5 V; 1.5 W
    b) 4 Ω   - 0.5 A; 2 V;   1 W
       2 Ω   - 0.5 A; 1 V;   0.5 W
       7.5 Ω - 0.4 A; 3V;   1.2 W
       30 Ω - 0.1 A; 3 V;   0.3 W

Standard Grade Physics 121

95. a) 12 Ω - 0.42 A; 5 V; 2.08 W
    60 Ω - 0.08 A; 5 V; 0.42 W
    4 Ω - 0.5 A; 2 V; 1 W
    2 Ω - 0.5 A; 1 V; 0.5 W
    12 Ω - 0.17 A; 2 V; 0.274 W
    6 Ω - 0.33 A; 2 V; 0.67 W
96. a) 3 A   b) 1.5 A
    c) 4.5 A
    d) 4 V
    e) 0.889 Ω
97. a) 1 A   b) 2 A
    c) 3 A   d) 12 V
    e) 4 Ω
98. a) 0.5 Ω   b) 40 Ω
99. a)

    b)

    c)

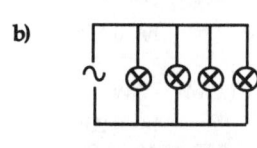

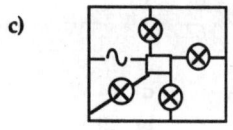

    d) parallel; other lamps stay on when one breaks.
    e) two paths for current, smaller current, thinner wire, less heat loss
100. a) 6 V; 18 W   b) 6 V; 6 W
101. 9 Ω, 3 Ω
102. 3 Ω, 6 Ω
103. a) 0.417 A   b) 1.25 A
     c) 0.625 A
104. a) 3 A   b) 13 A
     c) 50 A   d) 13 A
     e) 3 A   f) 50 A
105. a) 3 A   b) 3 A
     c) 13 A   d) 3 A
106. yes, takes 11.25 A
107. no takes 13.1 A
108. a) Fuse blows whenever switched on.
     b) allows far too much current therefore, no protection.
109. a) i) 10 units   ii) 80 p
     b) i) 2.625 units   ii) 21 p
     c) i) 0.325 units   ii) 2.6 p
     d) i) 0.0084 units   ii) 0.067 p
     e) i) 60 h   ii) 120 p
     f) i) 60 W   ii) 4.08 p
     g) i) 25 h   ii) 12.5 units
110. a) 7.5 p   b) 22.5 p
     c) 131.25 p
111. £10 .70
112. a) 3 600 000 J
     b) joule too small a unit
113. a) £1.81   b) 7.96×10^7 J
114. a) 70 533 J   b) 705 W J
     c) 0.02 units   d) 0.17 p
115. a) 286.5 p   b) £260.72
     c) £274.72
116. a) The battery can supply at 12 V, a quantity of electricty equivalent to 48 A for 1 h.
     b) 12 A   c) 13 A
     d) 4 h   e) £48.6
117. a) moves up   b) moves down
     c) moves down   d) moves up
118. a) does not move
     b) turns anti clockwise
     c) with a split ring commutator
     d) more turns; increased current; stronger magnets
     e) smaller; only one turn; permanent magnets not electromagnets.
119. a) 10   b) 20
     c) 75
120. a) i) current flows
        ii) soft iron at **B** becomes magnetic
        iii) **C** is attracted
        iv) contact broken
        v) current stops
        vi) **B** loses its magnetism
        vii) contact remade
     b) sound, as hammer continually hits gong
121. a) momentary reading in one direction
     b) zero
     c) momentary reading in the other direction
     d) since a.c. current
     e) directions of current reversed
     f) move magnet faster; more coils; stronger magnet
122. a) bob is moving fastest
     b) bob and wire momentarily still
     c) -40 μA   d) zero
     e) move bob faster

HEALTH PHYSICS

1. a) 100 °C   b) 0 °C
   c) 37 °C   d) 29 - 30 °C
2. a) 10 °C   b) 70 °C
   c) 10.5 cm
3. a) 96 mV   b) 335 °C
4. a) two pieces of metal joined along length
   b) metals expand at different rates
   c i) 29.4°   ii) 588 °C
5. a) 45 °C   b) -15 °C
   c) 155.5 mm
6. a) 0.017 m   b) 17 m
7. a) 22 kHz   b) 29 pupils
   c) i) 14 kHz
   ii) prolonged exposure to loud noise
8. a) 60 dB
   b) 140 dB
9. a) sound above range of human hearing, > 20 kHz
   b) 40 kHz hence ultrasound
10. 6.8 mm
11. a) B-reflected; C - refracted
    b) 50°, 30°C
12. a) 360 m   b) 180 m
    c) 144 m   d) 72 m
13. a) 250 000 pulses   b) 4 µs
    c) 7.5 cm
14. 67 µs
15. a) 0.2072 m; 0.1036 m
    b) 2.2 MHz   c) 0.67 mm
16. a) 1.25 MHz   b) 1500 m s^{-1}
    c) 80 µs
17. a) 1.3 MHz   b) 1500 m s^{-1}
    c) i) 7.5 cm
    ii) 7.5 cm
    iii) 19 cm
18. a) 1.28 MHz   b) 1474 m s^{-1}
    c) 0.88 m
19. a) f > 20 kHz, dog can hear ultrasound.
    b) anything above 20 kHz
    c) 18.9 kHz hence not ultrasound
20. a) [ray diagram: air to glass]
    b) [ray diagram: glass to air]
21. a) [concave lens diagram]
    b) [convex lens diagram]
    c) concave; convex
22. a) image at 30 cm, magnification 2
    b) image at 20 cm, magnification 1
23. a) image at 60 cm, magnification 1
    b) image at 90 cm, magnification 2
24. a) lens thin
    b) lens thick
25. a) long sight [eye diagram]
    b) short sight [eye diagram]
26. a) near objects clear, far objects blurred
    b) far objects clear, near objects blurred.
27. a) short sight
    b) concave lens
28. a) long sight
    b) convex lens

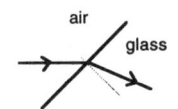

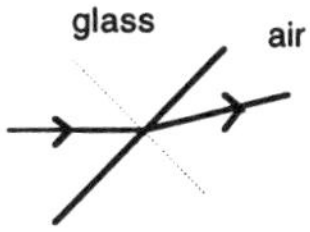

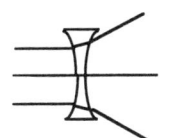

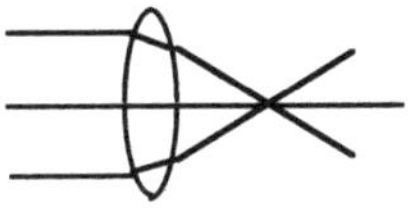

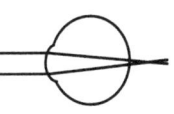

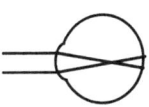

Standard Grade Physics

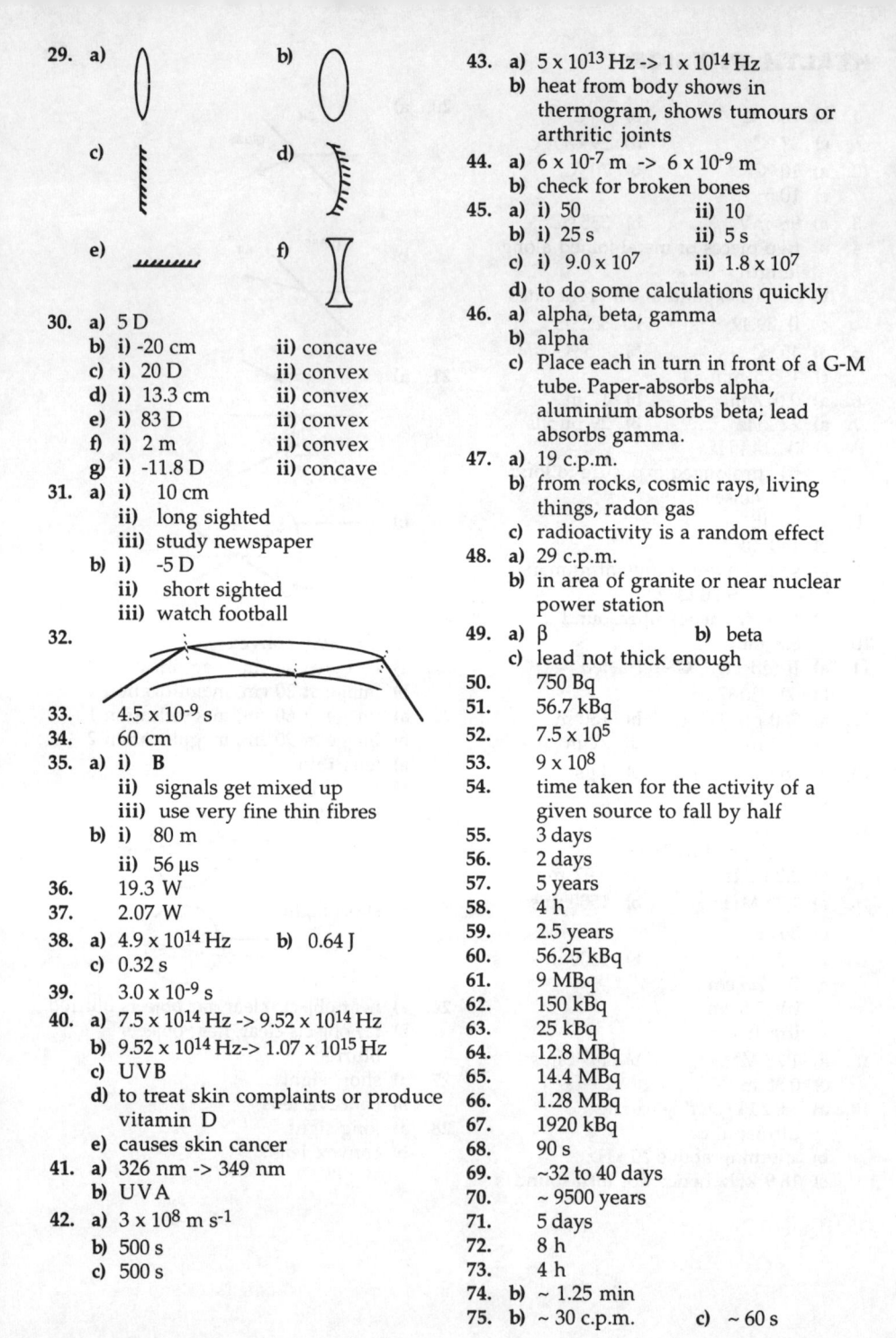

29. a) [convex lens]   b) [convex lens]
    c) [concave mirror]   d) [convex mirror]
    e) [plane mirror]   f) [concave lens]

30. a) 5 D
    b) i) -20 cm   ii) concave
    c) i) 20 D   ii) convex
    d) i) 13.3 cm   ii) convex
    e) i) 83 D   ii) convex
    f) i) 2 m   ii) convex
    g) i) -11.8 D   ii) concave

31. a) i) 10 cm
       ii) long sighted
       iii) study newspaper
    b) i) -5 D
       ii) short sighted
       iii) watch football

32. [diagram]

33. 4.5×10^{-9} s
34. 60 cm
35. a) i) B
       ii) signals get mixed up
       iii) use very fine thin fibres
    b) i) 80 m
       ii) 56 μs
36. 19.3 W
37. 2.07 W
38. a) 4.9×10^{14} Hz   b) 0.64 J
    c) 0.32 s
39. 3.0×10^{-9} s
40. a) 7.5×10^{14} Hz -> 9.52×10^{14} Hz
    b) 9.52×10^{14} Hz -> 1.07×10^{15} Hz
    c) UVB
    d) to treat skin complaints or produce vitamin D
    e) causes skin cancer
41. a) 326 nm -> 349 nm
    b) UVA
42. a) 3×10^8 m s^{-1}
    b) 500 s
    c) 500 s

43. a) 5×10^{13} Hz -> 1×10^{14} Hz
    b) heat from body shows in thermogram, shows tumours or arthritic joints
44. a) 6×10^{-7} m -> 6×10^{-9} m
    b) check for broken bones
45. a) i) 50   ii) 10
    b) i) 25 s   ii) 5 s
    c) i) 9.0×10^7 ii) 1.8×10^7
    d) to do some calculations quickly
46. a) alpha, beta, gamma
    b) alpha
    c) Place each in turn in front of a G-M tube. Paper-absorbs alpha, aluminium absorbs beta; lead absorbs gamma.
47. a) 19 c.p.m.
    b) from rocks, cosmic rays, living things, radon gas
    c) radioactivity is a random effect
48. a) 29 c.p.m.
    b) in area of granite or near nuclear power station
49. a) β   b) beta
    c) lead not thick enough
50. 750 Bq
51. 56.7 kBq
52. 7.5×10^5
53. 9×10^8
54. time taken for the activity of a given source to fall by half
55. 3 days
56. 2 days
57. 5 years
58. 4 h
59. 2.5 years
60. 56.25 kBq
61. 9 MBq
62. 150 kBq
63. 25 kBq
64. 12.8 MBq
65. 14.4 MBq
66. 1.28 MBq
67. 1920 kBq
68. 90 s
69. ~32 to 40 days
70. ~9500 years
71. 5 days
72. 8 h
73. 4 h
74. b) ~ 1.25 min
75. b) ~ 30 c.p.m.   c) ~ 60 s

ELECTRONICS

1. a)  [waveform: irregular analogue signal]
   b)  [waveform: square digital signal]
2. digital - switch, others are analogue
3. analogue - motor and loudspeaker, others are digital
4. a) loudspeaker b) LED
   c) 7 segment display
   d) solenoid
5. a) microphone b) thermistor
   c) capacitor d) LDR
6. a) i) fgbc ii) fabc
   iii) bc iv) abged
   b) 3
7. 450 Ω
8. 667 Ω
9. a) 1800 Ω
   b) 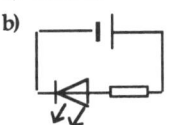 [circuit diagram: battery with LED and resistor in series]
10. a) 2 A b) 6 V
    c) 3 Ω
11. a) 3 A b) 12 V
    c) 4 Ω
12. 240 Ω
13. a) 3 A b) 204 V
    c) 68 Ω
14. 300 Ω
15. 1.5 Ω
16. a) motor only needs 475 V
    b) 5 Ω
17. a) 580 Ω b) 320 Ω
    c) 0.032 W
18. a) 3 V; 3 V b) 4 V; 8 V
    c) 2 V; 6 V
19. a) 1.73 V; 0.77 V b) 20.6 V; 51.4 V
    c) 13.3 V; 10.7 V
20. a) 10 V; 40 Ω b) 6 V; 50 Ω
    c) 4.2 V; 8.75 Ω
21. a) 550 V; 2700 Ω b) 12 V; 272 Ω
    c) 32 V; 1500 Ω
22. a) 8 V; 8 V; 8 V
    b) 167 V; 333 V; 500 V
    c) 25 V; 37.5 V; 12.5 V
23. a) 9.78 V; 7.56 V; 14.7 V
    b) 1.84 V; 3.16 V; 5 V
    c) 1591 V; 2273 V; 1136 V
24. a) 1.2 V; 3.96 V; 6.84 V
    b) 4.82 V; 0.29 V; 0.89 V
    c) 0.51 V; 3.75 V; 0.74 V
25. decreases
26. increases
27. b) i) ~300 Ω ii) ~420 Ω
    c) ~19.4 mA
28. b) i) ~260 units ii) ~650 units
    c) i) ~5.32 mA ii) ~9.09 mA
29. a) 8 mA b) 8.3 V
    c) 1.5 mA d) ~4 mA
30. a) 2.37 mA b) 3.21 mA
    c) 3.57 mA d) 3.75 mA
    e) ~3.9 mA
31. energy and charge
32. a) i) increased ii) increased
    b) i) 0.1 s ii) 100 k
    iii) 10 s iv) 10 s
    v) 100 s vi) 1 mF
33. b) 16 V, fully charged at supply voltage
    c) increase **R** or **C**
34. gives time delay, e.g. pedestrian lights
35. a) Voltage 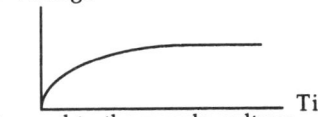
    [graph: rising curve approaching horizontal asymptote vs Time]
    b) equal to the supply voltage
36. a) transistor
    b) increases
    c) 0.7 V
    d) to protect the LED
    e) to adjust temperature when the LED switches on
    f) warning of temperature drop, e.g. in greenhouse
37. a) LDR
    b) decreases
    c) increases
    d) as it gets light
    e) swap variable resistor and the LDR
    f) as a warning light if too much light in a dark room

Standard Grade Physics

38. [circuit diagram with thermistor and transistor driving a buzzer]

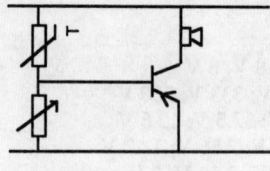

39. [circuit diagram with LDR and transistor driving a motor M]

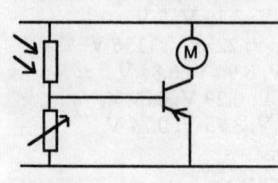

40. a) to discharge the capacitor
b) increases from zero
c) when V = 0.7 V
d) to vary time taken to reach 0.7 V
e) pedestrian lights

41. a) i) charged   ii) 0
       iii) 12 V   iv) off
    b) i) discharged   ii) 12 V
       iii) 0   iv) on

42. a) [NOT gate symbol]
    b)
in	out
0	1
1	0

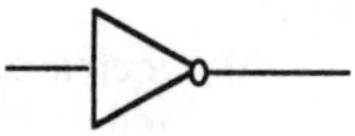

43. a) [AND gate symbol]
    b)
A	B	out
0	0	0
0	1	0
1	0	0
1	1	1

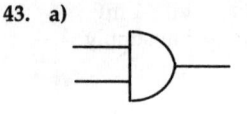

44. a) [OR gate symbol]
    b)
A	B	out
0	0	0
0	1	1
1	0	1
1	1	1

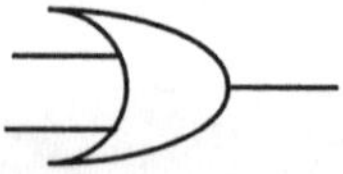

45. 0100
46. 1011
47.
D	E	output
0	1	1
0	1	1
0	1	1
0	1	1
0	1	1
0	1	1
1	0	0
1	0	1

48.
D	E	output
0	1	0
0	1	1
1	0	0
1	0	0
1	0	0
1	0	0
1	0	0
1	0	0

49.
D	E	output
0	1	0
0	0	0
1	1	1
1	0	0
1	1	1
1	0	0
1	1	1
1	1	0

50.
D	E	output
0	1	1
0	0	0
0	1	1
0	0	0
0	1	1
0	0	0
1	1	1
1	0	1

51.
A	B	C	D	E	F	G	output
0	0	0	1	1	1	1	0
0	0	1	1	1	1	1	1
0	1	0	1	0	0	0	0
0	1	1	1	0	0	0	0
1	0	0	0	1	0	1	0
1	0	1	0	1	0	1	1
1	1	0	0	0	0	0	0
1	1	1	0	0	0	0	0

52.
A	B	C	D	E	F	G	output
0	0	0	0	1	1	1	0
0	0	1	0	1	0	0	1
0	1	0	1	0	1	0	1
0	1	1	1	0	0	0	1
1	0	0	1	0	1	0	1
1	0	1	1	0	0	0	1
1	1	0	1	0	1	0	1
1	1	1	1	0	0	0	1

53. light sensor → [NOT] → [AND] → motor
temperature sensor →

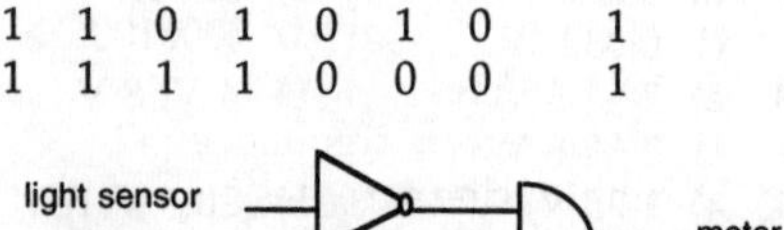

54. alarm → [NOT] → [AND] → [AND] → cabinet lock
main switch →
cabinet switch →

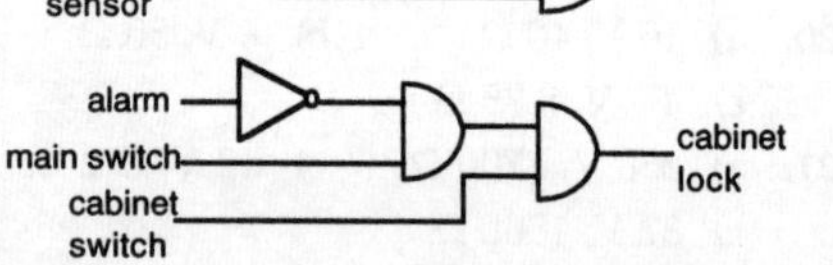

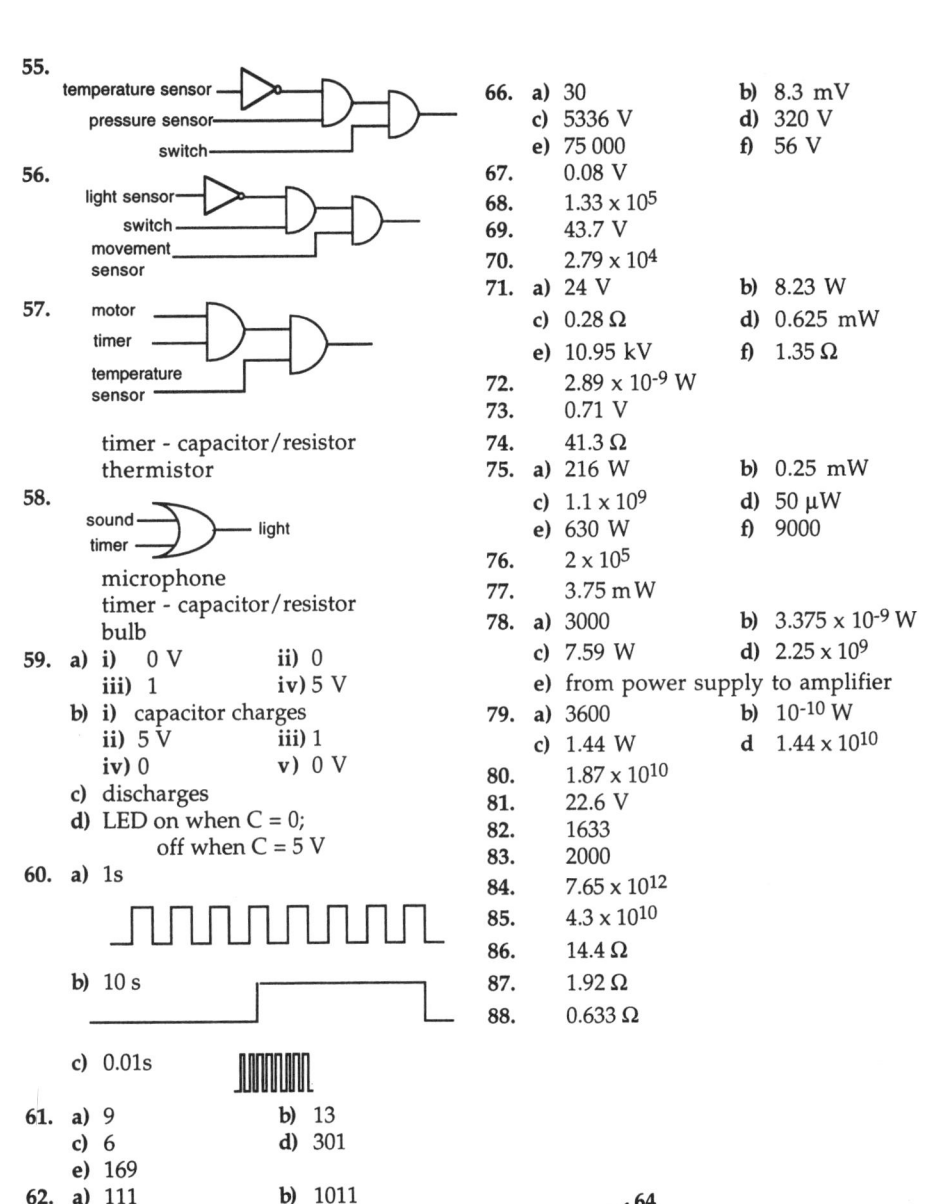

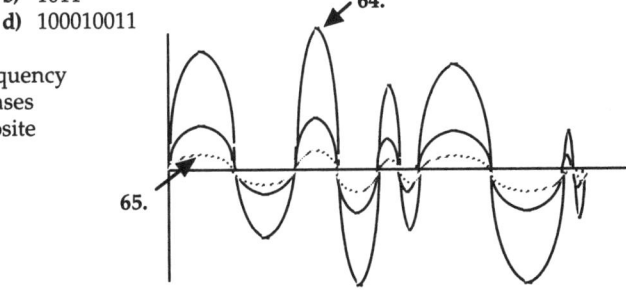

55. *[logic circuit: temperature sensor (NOT) → AND with pressure sensor → AND with switch]*

56. *[logic circuit: light sensor (NOT) → AND with switch → AND with movement sensor]*

57. *[logic circuit: motor AND timer → AND with temperature sensor]*

   timer - capacitor/resistor
   thermistor

58. *[logic circuit: sound, timer → OR → light]*

   microphone
   timer - capacitor/resistor
   bulb

59. a) i) 0 V   ii) 0
       iii) 1   iv) 5 V
   b) i) capacitor charges
       ii) 5 V   iii) 1
       iv) 0   v) 0 V
   c) discharges
   d) LED on when C = 0;
       off when C = 5 V

60. a) 1s

   [square wave trace]

   b) 10 s

   [single pulse trace]

   c) 0.01s *[rapid pulse trace]*

61. a) 9   b) 13
   c) 6   d) 301
   e) 169

62. a) 111   b) 1011
   c) 11111   d) 100010011
   e) 10110011100

63. a) no change in frequency
   b) amplitude increases

64. and 65. trace opposite

66. a) 30   b) 8.3 mV
   c) 5336 V   d) 320 V
   e) 75 000   f) 56 V

67. 0.08 V
68. 1.33×10^5
69. 43.7 V
70. 2.79×10^4
71. a) 24 V   b) 8.23 W
   c) 0.28 Ω d) 0.625 mW
   e) 10.95 kV   f) 1.35 Ω
72. 2.89×10^{-9} W
73. 0.71 V
74. 41.3 Ω
75. a) 216 W   b) 0.25 mW
   c) 1.1×10^9 d) 50 μW
   e) 630 W   f) 9000
76. 2×10^5
77. 3.75 mW
78. a) 3000   b) 3.375×10^{-9} W
   c) 7.59 W   d) 2.25×10^9
   e) from power supply to amplifier
79. a) 3600   b) 10^{-10} W
   c) 1.44 W   d) 1.44×10^{10}
80. 1.87×10^{10}
81. 22.6 V
82. 1633
83. 2000
84. 7.65×10^{12}
85. 4.3×10^{10}
86. 14.4 Ω
87. 1.92 Ω
88. 0.633 Ω

[waveform diagram for 64 and 65]

Standard Grade Physics

TRANSPORT

1. 16.7 m s^{-1}
2. 1.67 m s^{-1}
3. a) 66.7 km h^{-1}
   b) Average speed includes temporary stops and varying speeds, averaged over a long period of time.
   c) 25 m s^{-1}
4. a) 51.8 km h^{-1} b) 66.1 km h^{-1}
   c) 128 km h^{-1} d) 66.4 km h^{-1}
   e) 18.5 m s^{-1}
5. a) 84 km h^{-1} b) 90 km h^{-1}
   c) 81.6 km h^{-1} d) 71.4 km h^{-1}
   e) 19.8 m s^{-1}
6. a) i) 51.4 km h^{-1} ii) 56 km h^{-1}
      iii) 47 km h^{-1}
   b i) does not stop so often
     ii) 18.9 m s^{-1}
7. a) 4 h 45 min
   b i) 1074 km h^{-1} ii) 298 m s^{-1}
   c) 1200 km h^{-1}
   d) wind against going, with plane on return
8. a) 27.9 km h^{-1} b) 7.76 m s^{-1}
9. 2548 km
10. 8274 km
11. a) 3 m s^{-2} b) -30 m s^{-2}
    c) 5 s d) 12 s
    e) 7 m s^{-1} f) 98 m s^{-1}
    g) 12 m s^{-1} h) 86.8 m s^{-1}
12. 0.8 m s^{-2}
13. -1.3 m s^{-2}
14. 13 m s^{-1}
15. 21.1 m s^{-1}
16. 6 m s^{-1}
17. 700 m s^{-1}
18. 650 s
19. a) 13.9 m s^{-1} b) 5.6 s
20. 10.75 m s^{-1}
21. a) i) 2.4 m s^{-2} ii) 90 m
       iii) 9 m s^{-1}
    b) i) 9 m s^{-2} ii) 202.5 m
       iii) 22.5 m s^{-1}
22. a) i) 5 m s^{-2} ii) -6.25 m s^{-2};
       iii) 237.5 m iv) 17 m s^{-1}
    b) i) 5 m s^{-2} ii) -7.5 m s^{-2};
       iii) 127.5 m iv) 11.6 m s^{-1}
23. a) i) 2 m s^{-2}; 9 m s^{-2}
       ii) -10 m s^{-2}
       iii) 221 m
       iv) 18.4 m s^{-1}
    b) i) 2.5 m s^{-2}; 3.67 m s^{-2}
       ii) -1.5 m s^{-2}
       iii) 175.5 m
       iv) 10.97 m s^{-1}
24. a) stationary
    b) changing direction after 14 s.
    c) 5 m s^{-2} d) -10 m s^{-2}
    e) 295 m f) 12.3 m s^{-1}
    g) 155 m
25. a) 4 m s^{-2} b) -4 m s^{-2}
    c) 294 m d) 12.25 m s^{-1}
    e) 138 m
26. a) 10 m s^{-2} b) 40 N
    c) 3 kg d) 26 N kg^{-1}
    e) 2.85×10^{-3} N f) 237 kg
27. a) 95 000 N b) 10^{-6} N
    c) 0.27 N d) 10^{-5} N
28. a) 78.7 kg b) 37.5 g
    c) 0.01 g d) 68 900 kg
29. mass
30. a) 700 N b) 70 kg
    c) 266 N
31. a) 9000 N b) 900 kg
    c) 23 400 N
32. a) 1.5 kg b) 1.5 kg
    c) 5.7 N
33. a) 35 g b) 35 g
    c) 0.91 N
34. a) 38 N b) 38 N
35. 590 N
36. 23 400 N
37. balanced forces => constant speed (Newton's 1st law)
38. a) $12\,000 \text{ km s}^{-1}$
    b) no forces in space => constant speed
39. 23 N
40. 26 N
41. a) 0.975 N
    b) no friction
42. 1×10^8 N
43. 5860 N
44. 1150 kg
45. 15 m s^{-1}

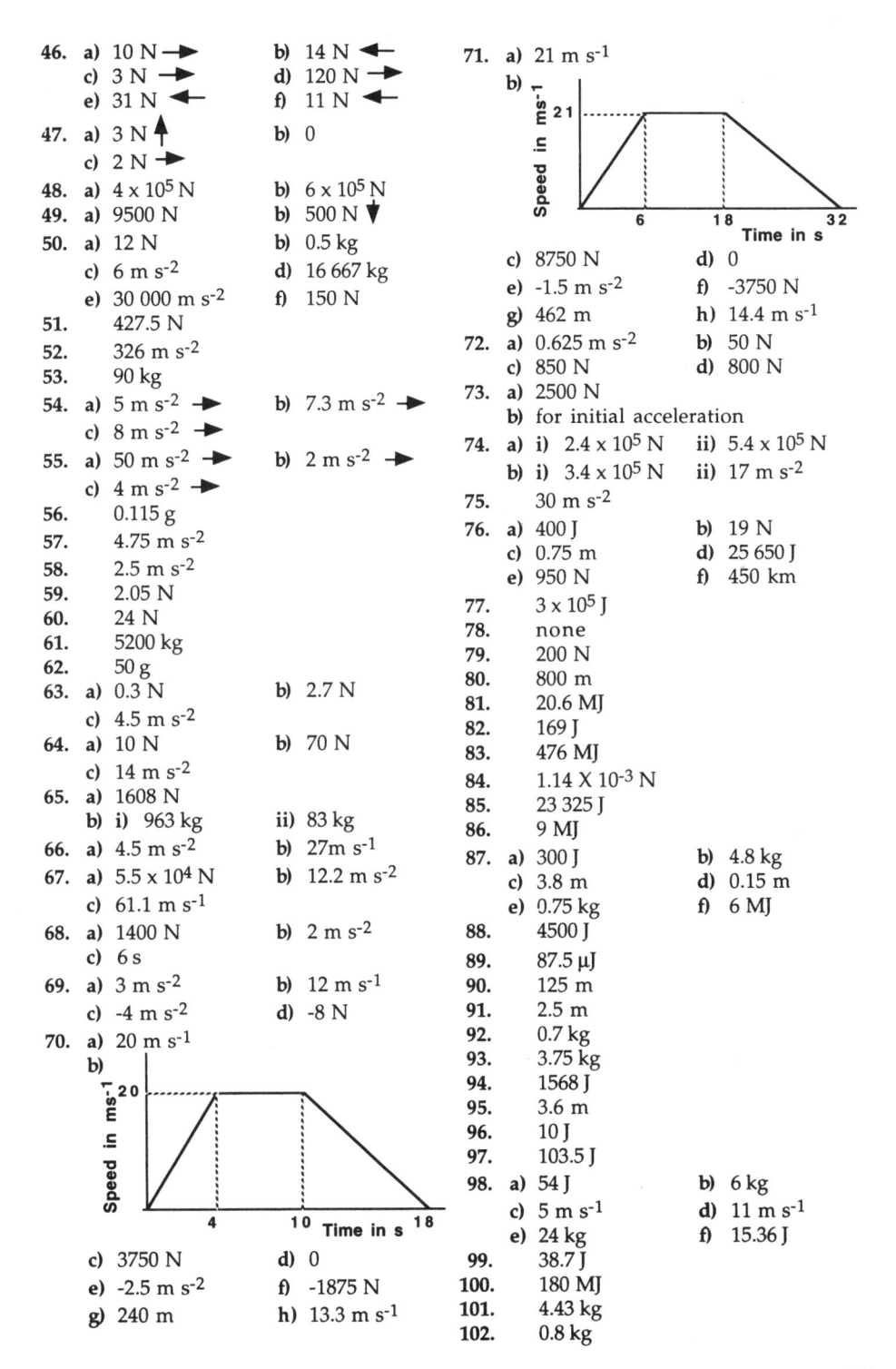

46. a) 10 N →   b) 14 N ←
    c) 3 N →   d) 120 N →
    e) 31 N ←   f) 11 N ←
47. a) 3 N ↑   b) 0
    c) 2 N →
48. a) 4×10^5 N   b) 6×10^5 N
49. a) 9500 N   b) 500 N ↓
50. a) 12 N   b) 0.5 kg
    c) 6 m s^{-2} d) 16 667 kg
    e) 30 000 m s^{-2} f) 150 N
51. 427.5 N
52. 326 m s^{-2}
53. 90 kg
54. a) 5 m s^{-2} →   b) 7.3 m s^{-2} →
    c) 8 m s^{-2} →
55. a) 50 m s^{-2} →   b) 2 m s^{-2} →
    c) 4 m s^{-2} →
56. 0.115 g
57. 4.75 m s^{-2}
58. 2.5 m s^{-2}
59. 2.05 N
60. 24 N
61. 5200 kg
62. 50 g
63. a) 0.3 N   b) 2.7 N
    c) 4.5 m s^{-2}
64. a) 10 N   b) 70 N
    c) 14 m s^{-2}
65. a) 1608 N
    b) i) 963 kg   ii) 83 kg
66. a) 4.5 m s^{-2} b) 27 m s^{-1}
67. a) 5.5×10^4 N   b) 12.2 m s^{-2}
    c) 61.1 m s^{-1}
68. a) 1400 N   b) 2 m s^{-2}
    c) 6 s
69. a) 3 m s^{-2} b) 12 m s^{-1}
    c) -4 m s^{-2} d) -8 N
70. a) 20 m s^{-1}
    b) *(speed-time graph: rises to 20 m s⁻¹ at t=4 s, constant to t=10 s, falls to 0 at t=18 s)*
    c) 3750 N   d) 0
    e) -2.5 m s^{-2} f) -1875 N
    g) 240 m   h) 13.3 m s^{-1}
71. a) 21 m s^{-1}
    b) *(speed-time graph: rises to 21 m s⁻¹ at t=6 s, constant to t=18 s, falls to 0 at t=32 s)*
    c) 8750 N   d) 0
    e) -1.5 m s^{-2} f) -3750 N
    g) 462 m   h) 14.4 m s^{-1}
72. a) 0.625 m s^{-2} b) 50 N
    c) 850 N   d) 800 N
73. a) 2500 N
    b) for initial acceleration
74. a) i) 2.4×10^5 N   ii) 5.4×10^5 N
    b) i) 3.4×10^5 N   ii) 17 m s^{-2}
75. 30 m s^{-2}
76. a) 400 J   b) 19 N
    c) 0.75 m   d) 25 650 J
    e) 950 N   f) 450 km
77. 3×10^5 J
78. none
79. 200 N
80. 800 m
81. 20.6 MJ
82. 169 J
83. 476 MJ
84. 1.14×10^{-3} N
85. 23 325 J
86. 9 MJ
87. a) 300 J   b) 4.8 kg
    c) 3.8 m   d) 0.15 m
    e) 0.75 kg   f) 6 MJ
88. 4500 J
89. 87.5 µJ
90. 125 m
91. 2.5 m
92. 0.7 kg
93. 3.75 kg
94. 1568 J
95. 3.6 m
96. 10 J
97. 103.5 J
98. a) 54 J   b) 6 kg
    c) 5 m s^{-1} d) 11 m s^{-1}
    e) 24 kg   f) 15.36 J
99. 38.7 J
100. 180 MJ
101. 4.43 kg
102. 0.8 kg

Standard Grade Physics   129

103. 9.5 m s^{-1}
104. 1.5 m s^{-1}
105. a) 20 m s^{-1} b) $1.8 \times 10^5 \text{ J}$
    c) from chemical energy in fuel
106. a) 21 m s^{-1} b) 61.2 kJ
    c) 187 kJ d) 126 kJ
107. a) $11\,580 \text{ m s}^{-1}$ b) $8.03 \times 10^{11} \text{ J}$
    c) stays the same; no forces acting
108. a) $144\,375 \text{ J}$ b) 640 W
    c) 3600 s d) 3 mW
    e) 400 J f) 175 s
109. a) 16.53 J b) 1.1 W
110. a) $18\,500 \text{ N}$ b) $18\,500 \text{ N}$
    c) 74 kJ d) 49.3 kW
111. a) 11.2 J b) 1.15 W
112. a) 9 m b) 5400 J
    c) 857 W
113. a) 8 m s^{-1} b) 1568 J
    c) 125 W
114. a) 19 m s^{-1} b) 172 kJ
    c) 821 W
115. a) 1040 J b) 1040 J
    c) 40 m s^{-1} d) mass
116. a) 13 m s^{-1}
    b) no friction, $E_p = E_k$
117. 1.25 m
118. 361 m
119. a) i) 4.8 m s^{-1} ii) 1.152 m
    iii) 0.8 m
    b) light gate at **A**, measure diameter of ball
120. a) 405 kJ b) 0
    c) 405 kJ
    d) 45 m
    e) Some energy is lost as friction.

121. a) 48.99 m s^{-1}
    b) Some energy is lost as friction.
122. a) $2.1 \times 10^5 \text{ J}$ b) 5525 J
    c) 38
123. a) 4.8 m s^{-2} b) 38.4 m s^{-1}
    c) 1843 J
    d) i) 1843 J ii) 230 N
124. a) 100 J b) 100 J
    c) 20 m d) 20 m s^{-1}
125. a) 216 MJ b) $2.88 \times 10^6 \text{ N}$
    c) $3.8 \times 10^5 \text{ N}$
    d) i) 28.5 MJ ii) 142.5 MW
126. a) $46\,000 \text{ J}$ b) 500 N
    c) $46\,000 \text{ J}$ d) 13.1 s
127. a) $11 \rightarrow 12 \text{ min}$ b) 0.167 m s^{-2}
    c) 195 N d) $365\,625 \text{ J}$
    e) 21.15 km
128. a) $18\,620 \text{ J}$ b) $57\,000 \text{ J}$
    c) $75\,620 \text{ J}$ d) 28.2 m s^{-1}
    e) i) $38\,000$ ii) $37\,620 \text{ J}$
    iii) 1254 N
129. a) $9 \times 10^5 \text{ J}$ b) 1 kW
    c) 1.17 MJ d) 1.17 MJ
    e) 190 m s^{-1}
    f) Some energy is lost as friction.
130. a) i) 1100 N ii) 1100 N
    b) i) 0.73 m s^{-2} ii) 11 m s^{-1}
131. a) 480 m b) 510 m
    c) 1 m s^{-2} d) 78 N
    e) 3900 J f) 156 N
132. a) 0.656 m s^{-2}
    b) i) 1.41 m s^{-2} ii) yes
133. a) 0.875 m s^{-1} b) $3 \times 10^{-4} \text{ N}$
    c) $2.63 \times 10^{-4} \text{ W}$

ENERGY MATTERS

1. oil, gas, coal

2.
Renewable	Non-renewable
Solar	Coal
Wind	Peat
Waves	Uranium
Hydroelectric	Gas
Geothermal	Oil
Tidal	

3. a) 1×10^6 J b) 1×10^9 J
   c) 5×10^5 J d) 4.5×10^{11} J
4. a) 48 MW b) 1.73×10^{11} J
5. a) 12 GJ b) 84 GJ
6. 3.84×10^{10} J
7. 9.26×10^4 W
8. a) 8.21×10^{15} J
   b) 0.42%
9. a) 2 MW
   b) 720
10. 50 MW
11. a) 20 b) 6 km²
12. a) 1.5×10^9 J b) 5.4×10^{12} J
13. a) 9 kg b) 32 400 kg
    c) 777 600 kg
14. 2000 A
15. 3250 A
16. 9.2×10^8 W
17. 1.33 GW
18. 120 s
19. a) 125 s b) 76.9 s
20. 20.3 kg
21. 26.8 kg
22. 17 kg
23. 28.6 kg
24. a) 1000 s b) 86.4 kg
25. a) 75% b) 180 W
    c) 340 W d) 1500 W
    e) 60.6% f) 624 kW
26. 20 %
27. 42 %
28. 37 %
29. 37.5 %
30. 50.75 MJ
31. a) energy lost in pipes, in turbines
    b) heat lost to atmosphere, energy lost in turbines
32. 548 MJ
33. a) 154 MJ
    b) energy lost as heat to surroundings and in moving parts of turbine
34. 2500 MW
35. 1220 MW
36. a) 0.108 s b) 8×10^5 kg
37. a) 1200 W b) 4.69×10^6 m²
38. 37.5%
39. a) 920 MW
    b) 2.36 GJ
    c) 84.2 kg
40. a) 1.28 GW b) 3.12 GJ
    c) 71 kg
41. a) 4.8×10^6 J b) 12%
42. a) $E_p \rightarrow E_k$ b) $E_e \rightarrow E_k$
    c) $E_k \rightarrow E_e$
    d) $E_c \rightarrow E_h$ (E_c - chemical energy)
    e) $E_c \rightarrow E_k$ f) $E_p \rightarrow E_k$
    g) $E_c \rightarrow E_k$
43. a) 2700 J b) 2700 J
    c) 60 m s^{-1}
44. all the same
45. a) 36 W b) 10 800 J
    c) 2160 J d) 20%
46. a) 200 s b) 8.1×10^5 J
    c) 74%
47. a) 84 W b) 39.7%
48. a) 4.5 kg b) 126 J
    c) 882 J d) 14.3%
    e) lost as heat to surroundings
49. a) stores E_e by pumping water back up to reservoir using unwanted capacity
    b) only way to store E_e
    c) at night
50. a) i) 770 kg ii) 1.155×10^6 J
        iii) 5.544×10^4 J iv) 1.21×10^6 J
        v) 6×10^6 J vi) 20.2%
    b) i) 5900 kg ii) 8.85×10^6 J
       iii) 4.25×10^5 J iv) 9.27×10^6 J
       v) 4.6×10^7 J vi) 20.2%
    c) i) 6×10^6 J
       ii) 2.3×10^6 J

Standard Grade Physics

51. a) 5.16×10^{13} J b) 108.5 days
    c) 5.5×10^6 J d) 3.03×10^6 J
    e) 5.5 MW
52. a) 25 turns b) 8 V
    c) 32 V d) 200 turns
    e) 12 500 turns f) 1.6×10^5 V
    g) 5.83×10^4 turns h) 11 kV
53. a) i) 26.25 V ii) 30 V
       iii) 44.1 V iv) 0 V
    b) a, c c) b
54. 7120 turns
55. 90 V
56. a) 300 turns b) 800 turns
    c) 180 turns d) 1120 turns
57. 800 turns
58. 2280 turns
59. 40 V
60. 0.25 V
61. 16.8 V
62. a) 18 V b) 0.67 A
    c) 27 Ω
63. a) 36 V b) 4.17 A
    c) 8.64 Ω
64. a) 50 turns b) 15 A
    c) 2 A d) 3200 turns
    e) 960 turns f) 1.125 V
    g) 4000 turns h) 10.9 mA
65. a) 0.4 A b) 1.15 A
    c) 8.4 A d) 2 A
66. a) 50 000 turns b) step-up
67. a) 37 500 turns
    b) step-down
68. a) i) 330 V ii) 800 mA
    b) i) 1.25 kV ii) 245 turns
    c) i) 14 V ii) 84 turns
    d) i) 800 turns ii) 18 A
    e) i) 507 V ii) 0.4 A
    f) i) 135 V ii) 1.07 A
69. a) 1.56 A; 5.6 V
    b) 240 turns; 2.3 A
    c) 52.5 V; 18 A
    d) 48 turns; 2.4 V
70. a) 134.4 kV b) 6.25 mA
71. a) 5 V; 90%
    b) 120 V; 81.25%
72. a) 16 V; 85.2% b) 168 V; 88.9%
73. a) 100 turns; 20.4 A
    b) 16 turns; 6.8 A
74. a) 1440 turns; 7.68 A
    b) 86 turns; 0.147 A
75. a) 72 V; 0.67 A b) 0.125 V; 40 A
76. a) 1200 V b) 1.5 A
    c) 7.5 V (each) d) 22.5 W
    e) 1185 V f) 118.5 V
    g) 15 A h) 7.9 Ω
77. a) 150 V b) 1.4 A
    c) 5.6 V (each) d) 15.7 W
    e) 138.8 V f) 27.8 V
    g) 7 A h) 3.97 Ω
78. a) 1800 V b) 0.4 A
    c) 3 V (each) d) 2.4 W
    e) 1794 V f) 89.7 V
    g) 8 A h) 11.2 Ω
79. a) 668 800 J b) 250 °C
    c) 400 J kg^{-1} °C^{-1} d) 0.25 kg
    e) 7875 J f) 2308 J kg^{-1} °C^{-1}
    g) 1018 kg h) 14 °C
80. a) 167 200 J b) 35 200 J
    c) 57 000 J d) 2600 J
81. a) 1.2 °C b) 4.5 °C
    c) 43.9 °C d) 2.9 °C
82. a) 0.239 kg b) 1.14 kg
    c) 2.63 kg d) 7.69 kg
83. 136 °C
84. a) 283 °C b) 178 °C
85. a) 201 s
    b) longer, energy lost to surroundings
86. a) 20 °C b) 25 080 J
    c) 760 J d) 25 840 J
    e) 517 s
87. a) 115.2 kJ
    b) 26.2 °C, assume all energy absorbed by aluminium
88. a) 355 300 J b) 444 125 J
    c) 222 s
89. a) 334 400 J b) 1.35 MJ
    c) 24.8%
90. a) 6 °C b) 2500 J
    c) 417 J kg^{-1} °C^{-1}
    d) too high, not all energy absorbed by copper
91. a) 2.08 A
    b) assume all energy absorbed by copper
    c) 52 W

92. a) 11.3 MJ b) 0.36 kg
    c) 25 000 J kg^{-1} d) 0.09 kg
    e) 1.12 x 10^6 J kg^{-1}
    f) 4.1 J
93. a) used to break bonds between molecules
    b) energy needed to change state of 1 kg without change of temperature
    c) fusion - change from solid to liquid
       vaporisation - change from liquid to gas
    d) *c* - energy to change temperature by 1 °C,
       L - energy to change state
       (both for 1 kg)
94. 8.684 x 10^5 J
95. 5.876 x 10^6 J
96. a) 1.336 x 10^6 J b) 1.672 x 10^6 J
    c) 9.04 x 10^6 J d) 1.205 x 10^7 J
97. 5.76 x 10^6 J
98. a) 9.3 x 10^5 J kg^{-1}
    b) too high, some energy lost to surroundings
99. a) as a control, to find mass of ice melted by room temperature without switching on heater
    b) 3.5 x 10^5 J kg^{-1}
    c) higher than accepted, some heat lost to surroundings or some water remains in funnel.
100. a) 223 s
     b) i) 1.41 x 10^5 J   ii) 82.6%
101. a) 0.225 m^3 b) 225 kg
     c) ~ 1.88 x 10^7 J   d) ~ 4700 s

102. a) AB - heat solid;
        BC - solid melting;
        CD - heat liquid;
        DE - liquid evaporating;
        EF - gas heating up.
     b) i) melting point,
        ii) boiling point
     c) takes more energy and thus time to evaporate a substance than to melt it
     d) CD
103. a) 800 J kg^{-1} °C^{-1}
     b) 48 000 J kg^{-1}
104. a) 8400 J; 6.68 x 10^4 J;
        8.36 x 10^4 J; 4.52 x 10^5 J;
        6.11 x 10^5 J
     b) 2.8 s; 22.3 s; 27.9 s;
        151 s; 204 s
     c)

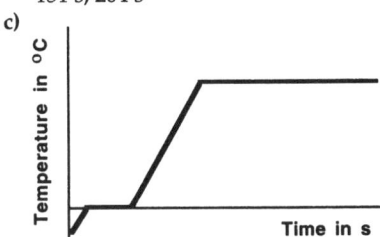

105. a) i) inside refrigerator
        ii) outside refrigerator
     b) 3 x 10^4 J   c) 2 x 10^4 J
106. 10 524 J
107. a) foil reflects heat back into room
     b) fibre glass is a good insulator, prevents conduction
108. a) 2.94 x 10^8 J
     b) releases energy on freezing which keep apples warmer
109. a) 84.8 °C
     b) energy used to keep body working
110. a) 47.8 g   b) 3 kW

Standard Grade Physics 133

SPACE

1. 9.46×10^{15} m
2. 500 s
3. 5.75×10^{12} m
4. a) 9.46×10^{19} km
   b) galaxy
5. 2008 light years
6. a) 9000 s b) 0.029 %
7. a) 1.28 s b) 4×10^{-6} %
   c) 1067 m s^{-1}
8. a) 8.5×10^{16} m
   b) 7.09×10^{13} s (2.25 million years)
9. a) 1.36×10^{8} s (4.3 years)
   b) 3.39×10^{13} s (1.075 million years)
   c) 1.36×10^{15} s (43 million years)
10. a) 6.3×10^{10} s (2008 years)
    b) 1.58×10^{16} s (502 million years)
    c) 6.3×10^{17} s (2×10^{10} years)
11. 10^{21} stars
12. 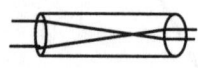
    b) X - objective lens, Y - eyepiece lens
13. a) 2 b) 2
    c) 2
    d) i) 15 x ii) 25 x
14. a) 84 cm b) 20 x
15. a) 93.5 cm b) 25.7 x
16. a) 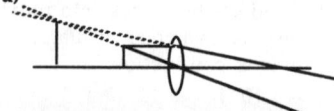
    b) upright, magnified, virtual, 6.3 cm from lens
17. a) 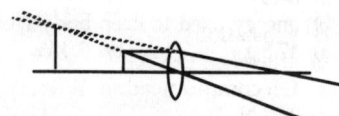
    b) 1.4 cm tall, 4 cm from lens, upright, virtual
18. a) 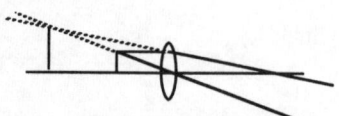
    b) 2.5 cm tall, 15 cm from lens, upright, virtual
19. a) i) 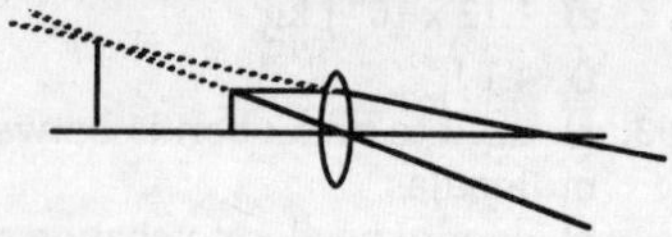
    ii) 2 cm tall, 4 cm from lens upright, virtual
    b) i) 
    ii) 1 cm tall, 8 cm from lens inverted, real
20. a) i) 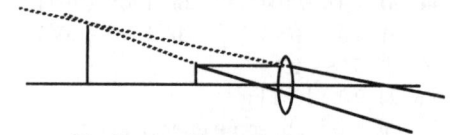
    ii) 5 cm tall, 20 cm from lens upright, virtual
    b) i) 
    ii) 1 cm tall, 10 cm from lens inverted, real
21. a) image same size as object
    b) image gets bigger
22. a) 4.29×10^{14} Hz
    b) 7.5×10^{14} Hz
23. a) 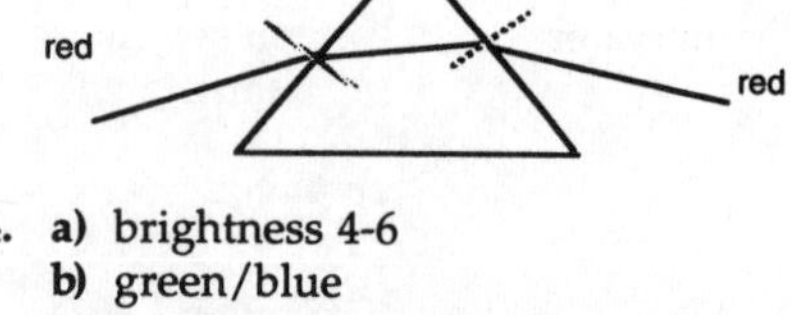
    b) 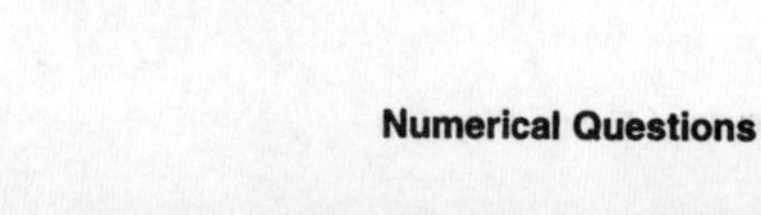
24. a) brightness 4-6
    b) green/blue

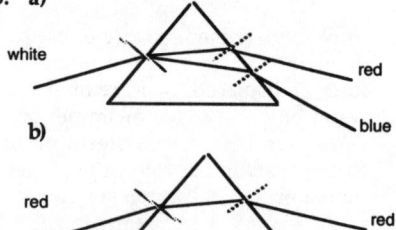

25. a) violet, indigo, blue, green, yellow, orange, red
    b) red, orange, yellow, green, blue, indigo, violet
26. a) 480 nm   blue
    b) 667 nm   red
    c) 588 nm   yellow
27. a) i) radio, TV, microwaves, IR, visible, UV, X-rays, γ-rays
       ii) γ-rays, X-rays, UV, visible, IR, microwaves, TV, radio
    b) travel at 3×10^8 m s^{-1}
28. a) 1.1×10^{13} Hz   b) 4×10^{-4} s
    c) 1.2 m
29. a) 273 nm   b) 500 s
30. a) 6.97×10^{-5} m   b) infra red
    c) phototransistor
    d) 300 000 s
31. a) 6×10^{-11} m   b) γ-rays
    c) Geiger-Muller tube
    d) 2.1×10^{27} m
32. a) 1200 m   b) radio
    c) aerial + radio
33. a)

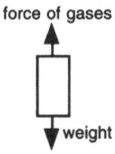

    force of gases ↑
    weight ↓

    force of rocket = force of earth
    on earth   on rocket
    force of gases = force of rocket
    on rocket   on gases

    b) upthrust ↑
       friction ← → thrust
       weight ↓

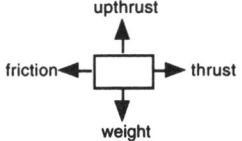

    force of swimmer = force of earth
    on earth   on swimmer
    force of displaced = force of
    water on   swimmer on
    swimmer   water (upthrust)
    force of swimmer = force of water
    on water   on swimmer
                        (thrust)

c)
    reaction ↑   reaction ↑
    [A] → F_{AB} F_{BA} ← [B]
    weight ↓   weight ↓

    force of skaters = force of
    on earth   earth on skaters
    F_{AB} = F_{BA}
    (force of skater A (force of skater B
    on skater B)   on skater A)

34. a) 27 N   b) 12 m s^{-1}
35. a) 200 N   b) 200 N
    c) opposite direction to that of ball
36. a)
    engine force ↑
    weight ↓

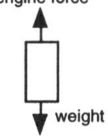

    b) 12 000 N   c) 9600 N
    d) 21 600 N
37. a) 112.5 N   b) 112.5 N
    c) 1.61 m s^{-2}
38. a) 375 N   b) 15 m s^{-2}
    c) 2.4 m s^{-1} d) 72 J
    e) 72 J   f) 28.8 N
39. a) 10 N kg^{-1} b) 450 N
40. a) 1.6 N kg^{-1} b) 104 N
41. a) 8.9 m s^{-2} b) 17 800 N
42. a) 3.7 m s^{-2} b) 7400 N
43. a) 55 kg
    b) i) 55 kg   ii) 203.5 N
    c) i) 55 kg   ii) 88 N
44. a) 700 kg
    b) i) 700 kg   ii) 1120 N
    c) i) 700 kg   ii) 2590 N
45. a) 77 N   b) 24 h
    c) geostationary
    d) allows constant telecommunication links
46. a) 139 N
    b) Both astronaut and satellite in free fall.

Standard Grade Physics

47. a) 2.5 s b) 2.5 s
c) 25 m s^{-1}
d)

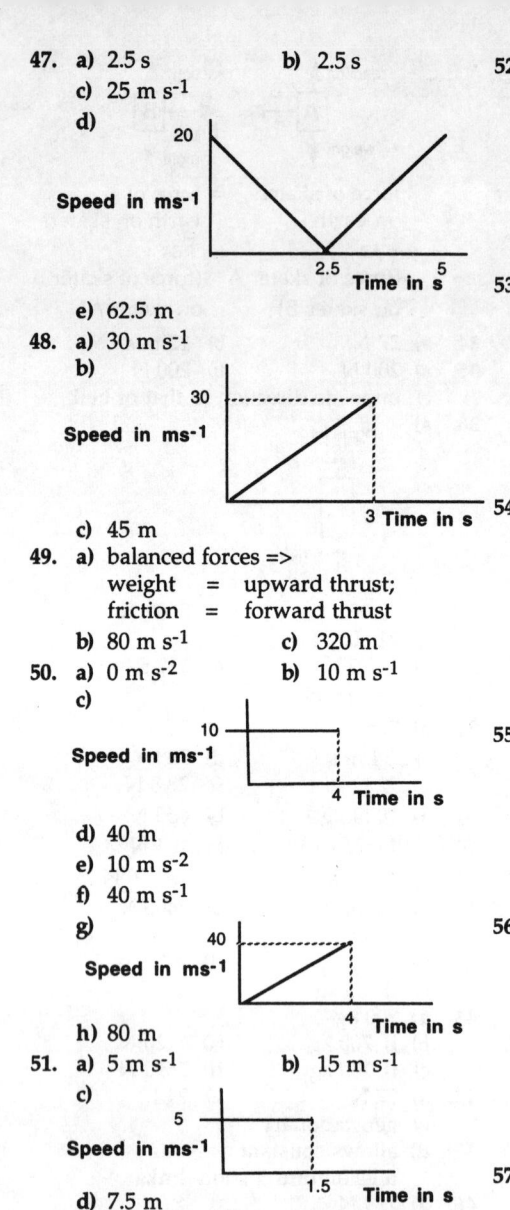

Speed in ms^{-1}, 20, 2.5, 5, Time in s

e) 62.5 m

48. a) 30 m s^{-1}
b)

Speed in ms^{-1}, 30, 3, Time in s

c) 45 m

49. a) balanced forces =>
weight = upward thrust;
friction = forward thrust
b) 80 m s^{-1} c) 320 m

50. a) 0 m s^{-2} b) 10 m s^{-1}
c)

Speed in ms^{-1}, 10, 4, Time in s

d) 40 m
e) 10 m s^{-2}
f) 40 m s^{-1}
g)

Speed in ms^{-1}, 40, 4, Time in s

h) 80 m

51. a) 5 m s^{-1} b) 15 m s^{-1}
c)

Speed in ms^{-1}, 5, 1.5, Time in s

d) 7.5 m
e)

Speed in ms^{-1}, 15, 1.5, Time in s

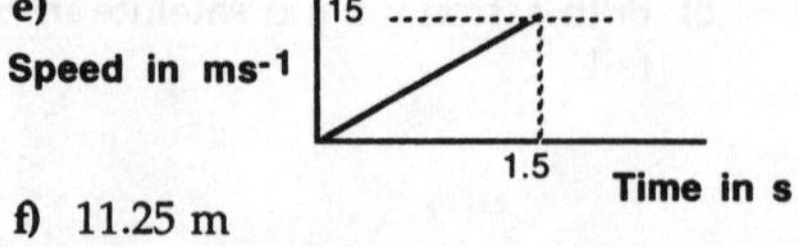

f) 11.25 m

52. a) 180 m s^{-1} b) 90 m s^{-1}
c) 1620 m
d)

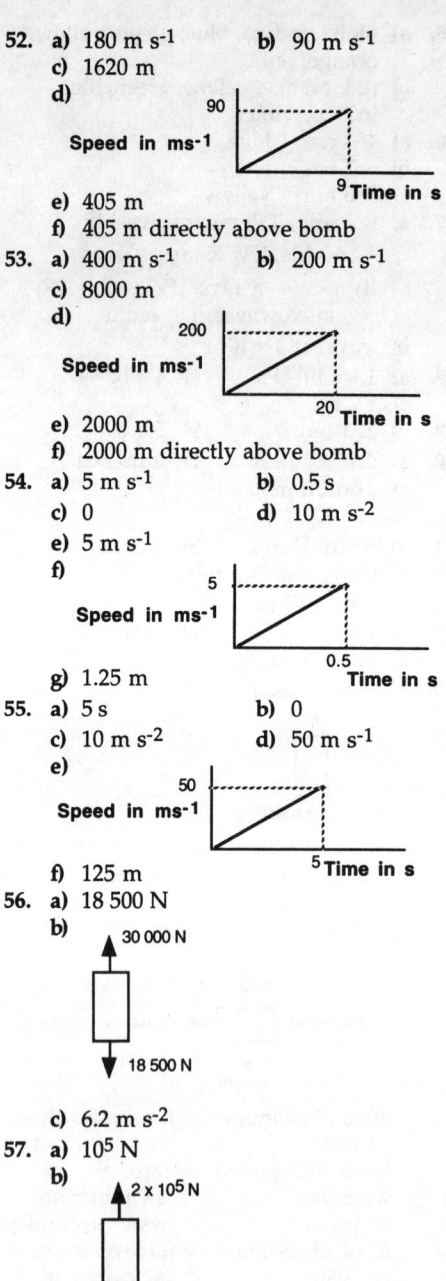

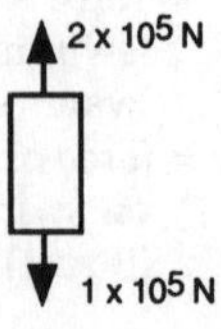

Speed in ms^{-1}, 90, 9, Time in s

e) 405 m
f) 405 m directly above bomb

53. a) 400 m s^{-1} b) 200 m s^{-1}
c) 8000 m
d)

Speed in ms^{-1}, 200, 20, Time in s

e) 2000 m
f) 2000 m directly above bomb

54. a) 5 m s^{-1} b) 0.5 s
c) 0   d) 10 m s^{-2}
e) 5 m s^{-1}
f)

Speed in ms^{-1}, 5, 0.5, Time in s

g) 1.25 m

55. a) 5 s   b) 0
c) 10 m s^{-2} d) 50 m s^{-1}
e)

Speed in ms^{-1}, 50, 5, Time in s

f) 125 m

56. a) 18 500 N
b)

30 000 N ↑, 18 500 N ↓

c) 6.2 m s^{-2}

57. a) 10^5 N
b)

2×10^5 N ↑, 1×10^5 N ↓

c) 10 m s^{-2} d) 7×10^4 N
e) 18.6 m s^{-2}

58. a) 66.7 s
    b) 4.5 GJ
59. a) 119 s   b) 6.48×10^{10} J
    c) 1108 °C
60. a) 3.96×10^8 J
    b) slows down due to friction with atmosphere
    c) 7.89×10^5 °C
    d) all material evaporates as so hot
61. a) 5.49×10^8 J   b) 6.88×10^5 °C
    c) much less as material evaporates from surface
62. a) 4.15×10^{11} J   b) 2.97×10^5 °C
    c) wing edges, nose and underside painted black, best radiator; shuttle covered with silica, good insulator.

63. a) 4.86×10^9 J   b) 3.38×10^9 J
    c) Fire **A** and **B** to slow down, then **C** and **D** to cancel deceleration.
64. a) 1.39 m s^{-1} b) 723 J
    c) 28.9 N
65. a) 5500 W   b) 1100 W
    c) 91.7 A
66. a) 6750 W   b) 1553 W
    c) 129 A
67. a) 4.38×10^{10} J   b) 1.09×10^8 J
    c) 291 N

GRAPHS

1. a) ***F*** = constant x ***a***
   b) 2.0 kg
2. a) ***d*** = constant x ***t***
   b) 0.2 m s^{-1}
3. a) ***E*** = constant x ***t***
   b) 4.67 W
4. a) ***V*** = constant x I
   b) 8 Ω
5. a) ***Ew*** = constant x ***d***
   b) 2 A
6. a) ***Q*** = constant x ***t***
   b) 0.25 N
7. a) ***Q*** = constant x ***t***
   b) 9.3 F
8. a) ***P*** = constant x $\frac{1}{V}$
   b) ***PV*** = constant

Standard Grade Physics